Academic

Orientation

For College Students

John Monyjok Maluth

Publisher
Discipleship Press
Web: discipleshippress.wordpress.com
Email: maluthabiel@gmail.com

Contact
Phone: +211 927 145 394
Phone: +254 797 624 994

ISBN: 978-1657758308
Library of Congress Control Number: 2022907038

DEDICATION

To students who are serious about education, even when life is not easy.
To the ones studying with limited time, limited money, and limited support.
To the ones who keep going anyway.

PREFACE

This book is for the student who wants to stop guessing.

Many students enter college with a good heart and a strong desire, but without the tools. They attend classes, write something, submit something, and hope the lecturer will be kind. That hope does not last long.

College rewards a certain way of thinking and working. It rewards clarity. It rewards evidence. It rewards discipline. It also rewards honesty, because academic work is not only about grades. It is about becoming a person who can be trusted with ideas and facts.

I wrote this book from lived reality, not from a perfect study room with perfect electricity and perfect Wi-Fi. I have done serious reading and writing under rough conditions. In Yei, I worked near Emmanuel Christian College where the power depended on a diesel generator and the internet was satellite. When the generator went off, the internet went with it. In Juba, I had no Wi-Fi. I used mobile data, and it depleted faster than it should. Sometimes I charged my phone from a laptop in the market, in heat and dust, then went home and worked for only a few hours. That kind of life teaches you something important: progress does not come from comfort. It comes from a system.

So this book gives you a system. Not a motivational speech. A system you can use whether you are in a quiet library or a noisy house. Whether you have a new laptop or only a phone. Whether your school is wealthy or struggling.

If you apply what is here, you will not only improve your grades. You will become a stronger reader, a clearer thinker, and a more honest writer. That is the kind of student who finishes well.

HOW TO USE THIS BOOK

Read it with a pen and a notebook. Digital notes are fine, but a notebook makes you slower in a good way. It forces you to think.

Do not read it like a story. Read it like training. After each chapter, take one idea and use it the same day. If you delay practice, you will forget the point and keep reading for comfort.

Keep one folder for your school life. Inside it, keep your course outlines, rubrics, lecture slides, and assignment instructions. Many students lose grades because they cannot find what they were given.

Lastly, do not treat academic skills as something only "smart people" have. These skills are learned. The difference is that some students learn them early, and others learn them late. This book is for learning them early.

WHAT SUCCESS LOOKS LIKE

- You can explain your course requirements in plain language.
- You can read an academic text and extract the main claim and the supporting reasons.
- You can turn a broad topic into a focused research question.

- You can plan a paper before you write it.
- You can write paragraphs that have one point, evidence, and clear logic.
- You can cite sources correctly and avoid accidental plagiarism.
- You can revise your work without hating yourself.
- You can study in a way that matches how exams are set, not how you wish exams were set.

QUICK START FOR YOUR FIRST TWO WEEKS

Week one is about setting your foundation.

Get every course outline and read it slowly. Circle the assessment items and deadlines. Write them into one place. If you do nothing else this week, do this.

Visit the library or the online library portal and learn what you can access. Most students wait until a deadline week, then panic. Do not do that.

Set a simple weekly rhythm. Choose fixed study blocks that you can keep. If your environment is unstable, create two rhythms: a power-on rhythm and a power-off rhythm. When you have power and internet, download readings, save webpages as PDFs, and send needed emails. When you do not have power or internet, read offline, outline your essays, and draft on paper or offline notes. This one habit can save your semester.

Week two is about building your core skills.

Choose one course and practice academic reading with one article. Do not aim for speed. Aim for accuracy. Identify the author's main claim, then list the reasons given. Write your own short summary in your words.

Choose one assignment and break it into steps. Do not start by writing the introduction. Start by understanding the question, collecting sources, and building your outline.

Write one page of practice writing. Not to submit. Just to train. A student who trains writing weekly will not fear essays.

CONTENTS

PART ONE

The University Learning System

College is not a place where you simply attend classes and hope your intelligence will rescue you. It is a system. A machine with rules, rhythms, and expectations. When you understand the system, you stop suffering unnecessarily. When you ignore it, you keep paying the same price in late nights, poor grades, and silent frustration.

I learned this lesson the hard way, not from a perfect campus library, but from real-life conditions where study time was limited by electricity, internet, and money. In Yei, I used Wi-Fi near Emmanuel Christian College, powered by a diesel generator. The generator could be switched off at any time. When power went off, the satellite internet went with it. In Juba, it became worse. No Wi-Fi. Only mobile data bundles that depleted faster than logic. Sometimes I charged my phone from a laptop in the market, a hot and dusty place, then went home with a few hours to read and write. That kind of environment does not allow fantasy. It forces you to build a system or fail.

This part gives you the system, in plain language, the way a serious student expects it. Not as motivational talk. As a way to think and operate.

1. The shift from school to university

In school, many students are rewarded for repeating. In college, you are rewarded for reasoning. That single difference explains why many students struggle in their first year. They enter with confidence, then the first assignment comes back with comments like:

- You did not answer the question.
- Your argument is unclear.
- Your sources are weak.
- Your references are inconsistent.
- This is descriptive, not analytical.

These comments sound painful, but they are not insults. They are signals. They are telling you that you have entered a different learning world.

In university, you are not mainly graded on how much you read. You are graded on what you can do with what you read.

You are expected to:

- Explain ideas clearly.
- Use evidence, not only feelings.
- Organize your thinking into structure.
- Show academic honesty through proper citation.
- Follow instructions exactly, not loosely.

This is why the student who "reads a lot" can still fail, and the student who reads less but works correctly can pass with strong grades. University is not only about effort. It is about method.

2. Academic culture and expectations

Academic culture is not something mysterious. It is simply the shared habits of serious learning.

Here are the expectations you must accept early.

You are responsible for your own learning

No one will chase you like a school teacher. You may be reminded, but reminders are not guaranteed. The course outline is the true reminder. If you do not read it, you are walking blind.

Claims must have support

In normal life, people speak with confidence and call it truth. In academic life, confidence is not enough. You must show why a claim is true, where it comes from, or how you reached it.

Clarity is respected

Many students try to sound intelligent by sounding complicated. That strategy fails quickly. Lecturers do not reward confusing language. They reward clean thinking expressed in clean sentences.

Academic honesty is not optional

If you borrow an idea, you name the source. If you borrow words, you quote and cite. If you paraphrase, you still cite. This is not about fear of punishment. It is about building a name you can respect.

A student who trains these habits early builds long-term confidence. A student who tries to shortcut them spends the semester in anxiety.

3. The university system as a small project

Your semester is not just time passing. It is a project with deliverables.

A project has:

- Tasks (readings, tutorials, quizzes, assignments, exams)
- Deadlines (submission dates, test dates)
- Quality standards (rubrics, formatting rules, citation rules)
- Resources (time, internet, library access, classmates, lecturers)
- Risks (power cuts, sickness, family obligations, work)

If you treat your semester like random daily survival, you will react to events instead of guiding your direction. If you treat it like a project, you plan, track, and deliver.

Here is the simplest semester control method I know.

Build one "semester page"

One page only. In your notebook or a document.

Write every course. Under each course, write:

- Assessment item
- Weight (%)
- Due date
- Submission method (online, physical, both)

That one page protects you from confusion. Many students fail because they cannot see their semester. They only see what hurts today.

Build weekly rhythm, not daily panic

Weekly rhythm is stronger than motivation. Motivation rises and falls. Rhythm stays.

Choose fixed study blocks per week. Even if you only do small blocks, keep them steady. When your study life is steady, assignments stop feeling like ambushes.

When my environment was unstable, I built two weekly rhythms, and it saved me.

One rhythm for power and internet.
One rhythm for no power and no internet.

That idea alone can change your life.

4. Learning spaces and class formats

University teaching uses different spaces. Each space has a purpose. If you misunderstand the purpose, you waste time.

Lectures

Lectures introduce direction, concepts, and structure.

Your goal in a lecture is not to write every word. Your goal is to capture:

- Main topic
- Key terms

- Core argument
- Examples used

What the lecturer emphasized twice

If you leave a lecture with a page full of sentences but no understanding, you wrote a lot and learned little.

Tutorials

Tutorials are practice spaces.

They test whether you actually read. They also teach you how to speak academically. If you arrive unprepared, you will feel lost and embarrassed. If you arrive prepared, you will understand faster and participate with confidence.

A simple tutorial habit:

- Before the tutorial, write one question from your reading.
- During the tutorial, ask it.

This habit turns you into a serious student in the eyes of lecturers and classmates.

Seminars

Seminars reward thinking out loud.

Seminars are not debates for ego. They are training rooms for reason. You are expected to contribute, but contribution does not mean talking too much. It means saying something that moves the discussion forward.

If you are shy, start small:

- Bring one written point.
- Bring one written question.
- Speak once.

Do that weekly, and your fear becomes smaller.

Labs

Labs reward accuracy and discipline.

Follow instructions like a contract. Many lab marks are lost through small careless steps. Also, lab reports have their own writing style. If your course includes labs, you must learn that style early.

Office hours

Office hours are an advantage many students ignore.

Office hours are not for begging marks. They are for clarity.

Bring one of these:

- Your assignment question, with your planned outline
- Your draft introduction and thesis statement
- Your list of sources, asking if they are acceptable

A short paragraph you want feedback on

A ten-minute office hour conversation can save you from writing a whole assignment in the wrong direction.

5. How grading works

Grades are not magic. They are built from criteria.

Most courses use a rubric. A rubric is not an enemy. It is a map.

If you want to improve fast, do this:

- Before writing, read the rubric.
- After writing, read the rubric again and check your work against it.

Many students do the opposite. They write first, then hope the lecturer likes it.

What markers commonly look for

Even across different courses, you will notice repeated categories:

- Understanding of the question
- Quality of argument
- Use of evidence and sources
- Structure and coherence
- Clarity of writing
- Referencing accuracy
- Depth of analysis

A strong paper is not only "well written." It is well reasoned, well supported, well structured, and properly referenced.

Feedback is not an insult

When your lecturer writes comments on your paper, do not read them like personal attacks. Read them like training notes.

- A student who uses feedback becomes better each semester.
- A student who ignores feedback repeats mistakes and stays stuck.

Here is a feedback method that actually works.

Make a "feedback list" for yourself. Every time you receive an assignment back, collect repeated issues into one list. For example:

- Weak thesis
- Too descriptive
- Poor paragraph transitions
- Weak sources
- Citation errors

Then choose one issue to improve in the next assignment. Do not try to fix everything at once. Fix one thing well, then move to the next.

That is how skills grow.

6. Academic communication

The way you communicate affects your academic life more than you think.

Email

Write emails with respect and clarity. Not long emotional stories.

A strong student email has:

- Clear subject line
- Course code and section
- Brief greeting
- One clear request or question
- A polite closing

If you attach a file, name it properly. If you send a draft, say what kind of feedback you want.

In-class communication

When you speak, speak with reasons. Avoid attacking people. Attack ideas with evidence.

If you disagree, use language like:

I understand your point, but I see it differently because…
Can we test that claim with an example?
What evidence supports that conclusion?

That is how academic speech works. It is firm but respectful.

Group chats and forums

Do not use group chats only for jokes and complaints. Use them for coordination and learning. Also, do not post careless messages. Screenshots travel.

A serious student protects their name.

7. Time, energy, and attention

Most students think their problem is intelligence. Many times the real problem is attention.

University demands sustained attention, and modern life attacks attention daily.

If you want to perform well, you must protect your attention like you protect your money.

A practical weekly plan

Choose:

- One day for downloading and organizing readings
- Three or four short reading blocks per week
- Two writing blocks per week
- One review block per week

This is not complicated. The power is consistency.

If your life is busy or unstable, shorten the blocks. Do not cancel the blocks. A small block done consistently beats a long block done once.

The two-rhythm method for unstable power and internet

This method came from lived reality.

When power and internet are available, do connection tasks:

- Download PDFs
- Save webpages as PDF
- Search for sources
- Send emails
- Upload drafts
- Back up files

When power and internet are not available, do offline tasks:

- Read saved materials
- Outline papers
- Write drafts in plain text
- Edit and revise
- Create exam recall notes

If you practice this, you stop losing days to power cuts. You stop saying, "I could not study because the internet was off." You study anyway, because you planned for reality.

I used this approach because I had no choice. In places where Wi-Fi depended on a generator, waiting for perfect conditions was not wisdom. It was self-deception. A system turned limits into progress.

8. Instructions are not suggestions

Many students lose marks because they treat instructions like general advice.

Assignment instructions often contain hidden marks. Not hidden in a secret way, but hidden in the sense that students ignore them.

- If the question says "compare," do not only describe.
- If it says "evaluate," do not only list.
- If it says "use at least eight scholarly sources," do not use three articles and five websites.
- If it says "use APA," do not mix styles.

A strong student learns action words. Here are a few common ones.

- Describe: tell what it is
- Explain: show how and why
- Compare: show similarities and differences
- Analyze: break into parts, show relationships
- Evaluate: judge using criteria, support with reasons
- Discuss: explore viewpoints and support your conclusion
- Critique: examine strengths and weaknesses fairly

When you obey the action word, you answer the question. When you ignore it, you fail even with good writing.

9. Participation as training

Participation is not noise. It is training.

Participation trains:

- Academic language

- Reasoning under pressure
- Confidence
- Listening

Question-building

Many students fear participation because they fear being wrong. But being wrong in class is cheaper than being wrong in an exam.

A simple participation system:

- Each week, write one question from each course.
- Bring those questions to class.
- Ask at least one.

Your questions do not need to be brilliant. They need to be honest and clear.

When you develop this habit, your lecturers see you as engaged, and you also begin to understand faster because your mind stays active.

10. Support systems you should actually use

University offers support, but serious students go after it. It does not fall into your lap.

Library

Learn the library portal. Learn databases. Learn how to search with keywords. If you can find sources faster than others, you will write stronger papers with less stress.

Writing center

If your university has a writing center, use it early. Do not wait until you are failing.

Bring your outline. Bring your thesis statement. Bring one paragraph. Ask for help with structure and clarity.

Study groups

A good study group is not a party. It is a training unit.

A useful study group has:

- Clear agenda
- Short time limits
- Practice questions
- Peer explanation

A useless study group has gossip, complaints, and unfocused talk.

Choose wisely.

11. Your academic identity

University shapes who you become. Not only what you know.

When you write assignments with integrity, you build a strong inner foundation. When you cheat, even quietly, you weaken yourself. You may pass an exam, but you lose something more important: self-respect.

The goal is not to become a "perfect student." The goal is to become a reliable thinker.

Reliable thinkers:

- Ask clear questions
- Use evidence
- Admit limits
- Cite sources
- Write cleanly
- Manage time
- Keep learning after failure

That kind of person succeeds in school, work, and leadership.

12. A short operating manual for the semester

If you want a simple set of rules to live by, here it is.

- Read the course outline in the first week and rewrite deadlines into one page.
- Start assignments earlier than your emotions say you should.
- Read with a purpose, and produce notes from what you read.
- Use rubrics before you write and after you write.
- Track sources from day one.
- Use office hours for clarity, not for drama.
- Build weekly rhythm, not last-minute hero stories.
- If power and internet are unstable, work in two rhythms and stop complaining.
- Treat academic honesty as personal dignity, not as fear of punishment.
- Respect your mind by protecting your attention.

Closing note for Part One

When students fail, the story they tell is often, "I tried." I do not doubt that many tried. But university does not only reward trying. It rewards working correctly.

When you learn the university system, you stop guessing. You stop wasting effort. You become calm because you know what to do next.

PART TWO

Research and Information Literacy

Many students fear research because they imagine it is only for final-year projects, or only for "smart people," or only for those who have unlimited internet and a quiet library. That belief is one of the biggest academic lies students carry into college.

Research is not a special club. Research is disciplined curiosity. It is the habit of asking, "How do we know?" and refusing to accept lazy answers. You use this habit in small ways every week, even in normal essays. The only difference between a beginner and an advanced student is how well they manage the process.

When your environment is difficult, research feels even harder. If your power is unstable and your internet is expensive, you cannot afford random searching. You must research with intention. I learned this while studying in places where the internet could disappear with the generator, and where mobile data could finish before your work is done. Under such conditions, you either build a working method or you keep losing time and confidence.

This part gives you that working method.

1. What academic research really means

Academic research is not "collecting information." It is answering a question using evidence, clear reasoning, and honest reporting.

In normal life, people believe claims because:

They heard it many times.
A friend said it.
It sounds right.
It matches their feelings.
It matches what their group repeats.

In academic life, those reasons are not enough. Academic work asks for something stronger:

What is the claim?
What is the evidence?
Where did the evidence come from?
How reliable is it?
What might be missing?
What limits exist?

Research trains your mind to slow down and become careful. It also trains your character. A researcher learns humility because the world is bigger than one person's opinion. A researcher learns courage because evidence can challenge comforting beliefs. A researcher learns honesty because academic work demands accurate representation of other people's ideas.

If you build these habits early, your assignments improve, your thinking sharpens, and your confidence becomes real.

2. Topic, question, and argument: the key difference

Many students confuse these three things and then they get stuck.

A topic is an area.
A question is a direction.
An argument is your answer.

Example:

Topic: "Education in South Sudan"
Question: "How does teacher absenteeism affect learning outcomes in rural primary schools?"
Argument: "Teacher absenteeism reduces learning outcomes by weakening continuity of instruction, lowering student motivation, and increasing dropout risk."

If you skip the question and jump from topic to writing, your paper becomes scattered. If you have a clear question, writing becomes easier because you know what you are trying to answer.

A useful rule:
If you cannot state your research question in one clean sentence, you are not ready to write the paper.

3. How to choose a topic without drowning

A good topic is not only "interesting." It must also be workable.

Choose topics using three tests.

Test one: Interest

If you do not care at all, you will procrastinate.

Test two: Access

Can you access sources on this topic? Do you have library access, articles, books, reports, or credible data?

Test three: Size

Can this be answered in the length you were given? A 1,500-word paper cannot solve a national crisis. It can study one slice of it.

If you fail the access test, you will suffer. If you fail the size test, your paper will become vague. If you fail the interest test, you will delay until it hurts.

Choose one topic that passes all three.

4. Turning a broad topic into a strong research question

A broad topic is like a wide road with no signposts. You can walk for hours and still not know where you are going.

To narrow your topic, use these focusing tools.

Focus by place

Instead of "healthcare," try "healthcare in Juba Teaching Hospital" or "healthcare access in Yei River County."

Focus by group

Instead of "students," try "first-year students" or "working students" or "students using mobile data for learning."

Focus by time

Instead of "in South Sudan," try "since 2016" or "during the 2020–2022 period."

Focus by factor

Instead of "poverty," try "transport costs," "school fees," or "food insecurity."

Then convert the focus into a question.

Weak question: "What is corruption?" Stronger question: "What factors increase the risk of procurement corruption in county-level public projects, and how can oversight reduce it?"

Weak question: "Why do students fail?" Stronger question: "What study habits predict poor exam performance among first-year students, and which habits show the strongest improvement when changed?"

A strong question is clear, focused, and answerable with available evidence.

5. The research problem and the problem statement

Students often write problem statements that sound emotional but unclear. A problem statement is not a complaint. It is a clear description of a challenge that needs study or careful explanation.

A problem statement usually answers four things:

1.   What is happening?

2. What is the problem inside what is happening?

3. Why does it matter?

4. What will this paper examine?

Here is a simple model you can follow.

1. Situation:
   Describe the setting in one or two sentences.

2. Problem:
   Name the specific issue.

3. Importance:
   Explain why the issue matters.

4. Focus:
   State what your paper will do.

Example shape:

Many university students rely on mobile data for study and assignment submission. However, unstable connectivity and high data costs can interrupt reading, research, and submission. This matters because disrupted learning often leads to late submissions, weaker writing, and lower grades. This paper examines how connectivity instability affects study routines among first-year students and identifies practical strategies students use to maintain progress.

Notice what this does.
It stays calm.
It stays clear.
It tells the reader exactly what the work is about.

6. Research objectives and research questions

Some assignments require objectives. Even when they do not, objectives help you stay organized.

Objectives are what you plan to achieve.
Research questions are the exact questions your work answers.

Example:

Objective:
To examine the relationship between study planning habits and assignment submission quality among first-year students.

Research questions:

1. What planning habits do first-year students use when preparing assignments?

2. Which habits are most linked to early drafting and timely submission?

3. What barriers prevent students from using these habits consistently?

When your objectives and questions match, your paper stays focused.

7. Types of research you will meet in college

You will hear research terms often. If you understand them early, you stop feeling lost in lectures and readings.

Qualitative research

This focuses on meaning, experience, and explanation using words.

Common methods include interviews, focus groups, observation, and document analysis.

Use it when your question asks:
How do people experience this?
Why do they behave this way?
What meaning do they attach to this issue?

Quantitative research

This focuses on measurement and patterns using numbers. Common methods include surveys, experiments, and statistical analysis.

Use it when your question asks:
How many?
How often?
How strong is the relationship between A and B?

Mixed methods research

This uses both words and numbers, often to balance strengths.

It can be powerful, but it can also require more time and careful planning.

For many undergraduate assignments, you will not collect new data. You will mainly use secondary sources. That is still research, because you are building an answer using evidence from credible work.

8. Secondary research and primary research

This distinction matters because students often claim they did "research" when they only read opinions online.

Primary sources

These are close to the original event, material, or data.

Examples:
A law document
An interview transcript
A dataset
A speech
A historical letter
A novel or poem you are analyzing

Secondary sources

These analyze, explain, or interpret primary sources.

Examples:
Academic books
Journal articles
Scholarly essays
Systematic reviews

A student mistake:
Building a paper on weak secondary chains.
One blog quotes another blog, and the student treats it like fact.

A safer habit:
When a claim is important to your argument, trace it back to a strong source.

If you cannot trace it, either remove it or state it with caution.

9. Where to find strong sources

If you can find sources well, you gain a serious advantage.

Start with your course materials

Reading lists are not decoration. Many lecturers build assignments around those sources.

Use your library system

Learn how to use the library search portal. Learn keyword searching. Learn filtering by year and peer-reviewed material.

Use academic databases

Your library often gives access to databases that you cannot access freely.

Use Google Scholar carefully

It helps you discover research, but some items are behind paywalls.

When you find a paywalled article, search its title in your library portal.

Sometimes your library has access even when Google does not show it.

Use citation trails

When you find one strong source:
Check its references to find older foundational sources.
Check who cited it to find newer sources.

This method is fast and powerful. One strong article can lead you to ten more.

10. Search skills: keywords that actually work

Many students search in full sentences and then wonder why results are random.

Academic searching works better with keywords and combinations.

Example:
Instead of searching:
"why do students fail university in first year"

Search:
"first-year university students academic performance predictors"
"study habits assignment submission quality"
"time management first-year students late submission"

Use synonyms:
"undergraduate" instead of "university student"
"academic achievement" instead of "grades"
"learning outcomes" instead of "results"

Use quotation marks for exact phrases:
"teacher absenteeism"

"mobile data cost"
"academic integrity"

Add location terms if your assignment is local:
"South Sudan"
"Juba"
"Yei River County"

When internet is expensive or unstable, searching must be efficient.

You do not search all day. You search in batches, download, then work offline.

11. Evaluating sources without being fooled

A source is not strong because it looks professional. A source is strong because it is accountable and evidence-based.

Use these checks.

Authorship

Who wrote it?
Are they trained in the area?
Do they show their qualifications or institutional link?

Publication place

Was it published in a peer-reviewed journal, a university press, or a respected organization?
Or is it a random website?

Evidence

Does the author cite other work?
Do they explain methods?
Do they show data or clear reasoning?

Purpose

Is it trying to inform, sell, attack, or recruit?
Purpose shapes how information is presented.

Balance and limits

Does the author acknowledge limits?
Serious academic work admits limits.

A student trap:
Using sources that confirm feelings instead of sources that
prove claims.

You can still hold strong opinions, but your paper must be
built on evidence, not on mood.

12. Reading sources like a scholar, not a collector

Some students treat sources like stones.
They collect many quotes and then throw them into a
paper.

That creates a paper filled with other people's voices and
no clear mind behind it.

Read sources with questions.

What is the author's main claim?
What reasons support the claim?

What evidence supports the reasons?
What does the author assume?
What does the author admit as a limit?
How does this help my research question?

When you read this way, your writing becomes yours.
You stop hiding behind quotations.
You start building a real argument.

13. Note-taking for research: the "source note" method

Bad referencing is often not a moral issue.
It is a tracking issue.

Students lose details, then panic near submission, then guess citations or leave them out.

Fix it early with one habit: source notes.

For every source you read, create one short source note with:

Full reference details (author, year, title, journal or publisher)
Main claim (one or two sentences)
Key points that matter to your paper (3–5 bullets or short lines)
Useful page numbers (if you may cite)
How it connects to your argument
One quote only if it is truly special

This makes writing easier because your future self is not hunting for lost pages.

If you have weak internet, this method becomes even more valuable.
You can work offline because your notes carry the key information.

14. Citation managers and simple systems that still work

Citation tools are helpful, but they are not your brain.

If you use a citation manager, still check the output.
Tools make mistakes with capitalization, italics, and missing details.

If you do not use a tool, you can still build a strong system.

Use a research folder with:

A "Sources" document where you paste full reference details
A "Notes" document where you store your source notes
A "Draft" document where you write

Name your saved PDFs in a clear way:
Author-Year-ShortTitle

Example:
Smith-2021-StudentTimeManagement.pdf

This simple practice saves hours.

15. Avoiding plagiarism and accidental plagiarism

Plagiarism is not only copying.
It can also happen through carelessness.

Common student problems:

Copying sentences and changing a few words
Copying structure and sentence shape too closely
Paraphrasing without citation
Using a quote without quotation marks
Using an idea as if it is your own

The fix is not fear. The fix is method.

If you use another person's words, quote and cite.
If you use another person's idea, paraphrase in your own
words and cite.
If you are unsure, cite.

Academic honesty is a form of dignity.
A student who respects sources respects themselves.

16. Building a small literature review without panic

Even when your assignment does not ask for a literature
review, you are doing a small version of it whenever you
use multiple sources.

A literature review is not a list of summaries.
It is a conversation map.

A simple way to build it:

1. Group sources by themes
    For example:
    "Causes of late submission"
    "Time management habits"
    "Impact of feedback"
    "Digital access and study routines"

2. Show agreement
   What do most sources support?

3. Show disagreement
   Where do sources differ?

4. Show gaps
   What is still unclear or under-studied?

5. Place your paper
   Explain how your paper fits: what it will focus on and why.

A beginner mistake:
Reading too many sources shallowly.
A better habit:
Choose fewer strong sources and read them carefully.

Quality beats quantity.

17. Writing a research plan you can actually follow

A research plan does not need to be complex. It needs to be realistic.

Here is a plan that works for most undergraduate assignments.

Step 1: Understand the question

Rewrite the assignment question in your own words. Underline the action word: analyze, evaluate, compare, discuss.

Step 2: Build your working question

Turn the topic into a research question.

Step 3: Collect sources in one session

Do not search for sources every day.
Search in one focused session, download what you need,
save the details.

This matters even more when internet is unreliable.

Step 4: Take source notes

Create source notes for each key source.

Step 5: Build your outline

Write your sections.
Assign sources to each section.
If a section has no sources, either find support or remove
the section.

Step 6: Draft

Write quickly but clearly.
Do not chase perfection on the first pass.

Step 7: Revise and reference-check

Check structure, clarity, and evidence.
Then check citations and references.

This plan sounds simple, but it is powerful because it
removes guessing.

18. Ethics in research and writing

Ethics is not only for science labs.
Ethics is for any student handling people's ideas and people's lives.

If you write about communities, write with respect.
If you write about conflict, poverty, displacement, or trauma, do not use suffering like decoration.

If you conduct interviews or surveys for a course project:
Get consent.
Explain purpose clearly.
Protect identity where needed.
Do not promise what you cannot deliver.

The world already has enough careless writers.
Academic training should make you a careful one.

19. Research under limited resources: a survival method that still produces quality

If you have stable internet and stable power, research is easier.
If you do not, research can still be done well, but you must change your habits.

Here is what worked for me when conditions were not friendly.

Batch your online work

Use internet time to:
Search and download
Email and upload
Back up files

Do not waste internet time reading long materials online.
Download and read offline.

Build offline strength

When the internet is off:
Read PDFs you saved
Write outlines
Draft sections
Edit and improve paragraphs

You do not need perfect conditions to produce strong work.
You need a method that respects reality.

20. Practice section: build your research question and mini source plan today

Do this now, even if you are not writing an assignment today.

1. Choose one topic you care about.
2. Narrow it by place, group, time, or factor.
3. Write three possible research questions.
4. Choose the most answerable one.
5. Write a short problem statement (4 sentences).
6. List five keywords you would search.
7. Decide where you would search first (library portal, database, Google Scholar).
8. Write the titles of three sources you already know or expect to find.

This exercise trains your research muscle.
The more you train it, the less research will scare you.

Closing note for Part Two

Research is not something you do once in final year.
It is a habit you practice every week.

When you can turn a topic into a question, find strong
sources, evaluate them honestly, take clean notes, and build
an argument with evidence, your academic life changes.

You stop writing from panic.
You start writing from preparation.

PART THREE

Academic reading and note-taking

Why academic reading feels hard

Academic reading feels hard for a simple reason. It is not written to entertain you. It is written to explain, defend, or challenge an idea. Many academic writers assume their reader already knows the basic terms of the field. So they do not slow down for you. They build on earlier debates, earlier studies, and earlier definitions.

A student meets that kind of writing and thinks, "Maybe I am not smart." That thought is a trap. The issue is not your brain. The issue is that nobody trained you in how to read this kind of material.

In school, you often read to finish. In college, you read to extract meaning and to use it in your own work. Those are different tasks. If you use school-reading habits in college, you will waste time, get tired, and still not understand.

Academic reading is a skill you build. You build it the same way you build strength. You start with smaller loads, you train consistently, and you recover. If you expect yourself to lift a heavy load on day one, you will feel pain and think you are weak. You are not weak. You are untrained.

Reading   with   purpose
If you start reading without a purpose, your mind will wander. You will underline many lines and remember nothing.

Before you open a chapter or an article, ask yourself what you need from it. Are you reading for a lecture tomorrow, for a tutorial discussion, for an essay argument, for a research project, or for an exam?

Your purpose changes what you look for.

When you read for a lecture, you want the main ideas and key terms, so you can follow the lecturer without feeling lost.

When you read for an essay, you want claims and evidence you can use, plus how the author defines terms.

When you read for a research project, you want methods, findings, limitations, and how the study connects to your question.

When you read for an exam, you want the structure of ideas and how they relate, because exams reward recall and explanation, not just exposure.

A purpose is also your time guard. A student with weak internet or unstable power cannot read aimlessly. You must read with direction so you can use your time well. I learned this under real conditions. When your power comes from a generator, you do not waste the hours when the lights are on. When you rely on mobile data that runs out too fast, you do not click around for fun. You download, then you work.

Three kinds of reading you will do as a student You will do self-chosen reading, course-required reading, and assessment-critical reading.

Self-chosen reading is the reading you do because you want to grow. It builds vocabulary, patience, and curiosity. It also builds a relationship with books that is not tied to grades. This matters because students who only read for grades burn out fast.

Course-required reading is the reading your lecturer expects you to do to follow the course. It may not be directly tested, but it shapes your understanding.

Assessment-critical reading is the reading you must do to answer an assignment or pass an exam. It includes key texts, key articles, and anything your lecturer repeats often in class.

Do not treat all three the same way. Self-chosen reading can be slower and reflective. Course-required reading should be steady and consistent. Assessment-critical reading must be targeted. If you treat everything as assessment-critical, you will drown. If you treat assessment-critical reading like casual reading, you will miss marks.

Skimming, scanning, and close reading
Many students think reading means starting at the first line and ending at the last line. That is one type of reading, but it is not the only type.

Skimming is fast reading for structure. You look at headings, subheadings, introductions, conclusions, topic sentences, diagrams, and summary sections. Skimming answers, "What is this text about, and how is it organized?"

Scanning is fast searching for specific items. You look for keywords, dates, names, definitions, examples, and references. Scanning answers, "Where is the exact detail I need?"

Close reading is slow reading for meaning. You stop and ask questions. You translate the author's sentence into your own words. You identify the claim, the reason, and the evidence. Close reading answers, "What is the author really saying, and why?"

You need all three. Skimming helps you avoid getting lost. Scanning helps you work efficiently. Close reading helps you understand.

If you try to close-read everything, you will hate reading. If you only skim, you will feel confident until the exam or assignment exposes you. Balance is the skill.

How to approach a journal article without fear A journal article looks intimidating because it is dense and because it has a strict structure. The good news is that the structure helps you.

Start with the title. Ask what it promises.

Then read the abstract. The abstract is the author's short explanation of what they did and what they found.

Then go to the introduction. The introduction tells you the problem, why it matters, and what the author is trying to do.

Then check the method and the data source. Even if you do not understand every detail, you must know what kind of evidence the author used.

Then read the findings or results. What did they discover?

Then read the discussion or conclusion. How does the author interpret the findings? What limitations do they admit? What do they suggest next?

After you do that, go back and read more carefully the sections that matter for your assignment. This approach stops you from drowning in the middle of page two.

Many students waste time because they read an article from beginning to end like a story. A journal article is not a story. It is an argument built on evidence. You must read it like you are checking a claim.

How to approach a textbook chapter Textbooks are designed to teach. They usually have headings, definitions, examples, and review sections.

Start by skimming the chapter. Look at headings and any summaries. Ask what the chapter is trying to teach.

Then read the introduction and the conclusion first. This gives you a map.

Then read section by section. After each section, pause and write one or two sentences in your own words. If you cannot write it, you did not understand it yet.

If you are reading for an exam, do not only underline. Underlining is weak if you do not convert it into recall.

Close the book and explain the section out loud or in writing. If you can explain it, you own it.

How to approach reports and policy documents
Reports and policy documents often contain useful facts, but they can be long and filled with formal language.

Start with the executive summary, if it exists. Then go to the section that relates to your topic. Use scanning for keywords. Look at tables and figures. But do not abuse tables. A table without explanation can mislead you.

When you take notes from reports, always record the report title, year, and the page number for key details. Reports are often updated, and your reader may need to trace your source.

Also pay attention to who produced the report and why. Some reports exist to inform. Others exist to persuade. You can still use persuasive reports, but you must read them with care.

Reading lectures and slides
Lecture slides are not full notes. They are cues.

If you rely only on slides, your understanding will be shallow. Slides usually contain keywords, not explanations.

When you receive slides, turn them into your own notes. Expand each point in your own words based on what the lecturer said. If you missed a lecture, do not only read the slides. Ask a classmate what was explained, or go to the lecturer's recording if available, then write your own summary.

The students who succeed are not the ones with the biggest piles of slides. They are the ones who turn those slides into usable knowledge.

Active reading without pretending
Some advice about active reading sounds nice but does not tell you what to do.

Active reading means you interact with the text. You ask questions, you identify claims, you mark confusion, and you respond.

Here is what interaction looks like in real life.

You write a question mark in the margin when a sentence is unclear.

You circle key terms and write simple definitions in your own words.

You underline a claim and write, "This is the main point."

You write, "Evidence?" when the author makes a strong statement without support.

You write, "Example?" when a section is too abstract.

You write, "So what?" when you cannot see why a point matters.

You write, "This supports my paper because…" when a section is useful.

This is not decoration. It is thinking on paper.

If you do this regularly, your reading stops being a struggle against the author. It becomes a conversation.

Handling hard vocabulary and long sentences
Many academic texts use long sentences and uncommon words. Students panic and assume they must look up every word. That can slow you down too much.

Use a smarter approach.

First, try to understand the sentence without looking anything up. Often, you can infer the meaning from the surrounding lines.

Second, if one word is blocking you, look it up. Write a short meaning in your notes. Do not copy a dictionary paragraph.

Third, build your own small vocabulary list for each course. Courses often repeat the same key terms. Once you learn those terms, reading becomes easier.

Fourth, break long sentences into smaller parts. Read the sentence and find the subject, the verb, and the object. Ask, "Who is doing what?" Then ask, "Why?" This simple habit saves you in many disciplines.

Also remember that some academic writing is poorly written. Do not assume every difficult sentence is deep. Sometimes it is just unclear writing. In that case, your job is to extract the best meaning you can, then move on.

The difference between highlighting and learning
Highlighting makes you feel like you are studying. But

highlighting is not learning unless it leads to recall and explanation.

If you highlight, you must do something next. You must convert highlights into notes, summaries, or questions.

A practical rule is this. If you highlight a paragraph, you must write one sentence that captures what the paragraph is saying. If you cannot do that, your highlight is only ink.

Notes: why most students take notes that fail

Most student notes fail for two reasons.

They are too long. The student tries to copy the book, and the notes become another book.

Or they are too short. The student writes keywords with no explanation, and later they cannot remember what the keywords meant.

Good notes are a bridge between the text and your brain. They are short enough to review, but full enough to remind you of meaning.

Notes should answer, "What is the point, and how do I explain it?"

A simple note structure that works in many subjects When you read a section, your note should capture these items in plain language.

The main idea.

The key terms, with simple meanings.

The author's key claim, if there is one.

The author's reasons or evidence.

Your response, question, or connection to your assignment.

This keeps your notes alive. They are not only storage. They are thinking.

Cornell notes without making it complicated

Cornell notes are useful because they separate details from prompts.

On the left side, you write cues, keywords, or questions.

On the right side, you write the explanation.

At the bottom, you write a short summary.

This method is powerful because the left side becomes a practice tool. When you revise, you cover the right side and try to answer the cue. That turns reading into recall.

If you are using a digital tool, you can still do Cornell style by using two columns or by writing questions first, then answers.

Outline notes for heavy chapters

Outline notes are good when a chapter has clear headings.

You write the heading, then under it you write the subpoints. You keep the structure of the text, but you rewrite in your own words.

Outline notes help you see the logic. They also help when you need to write an essay because essays also need structure.

Mind maps for relationships

Some subjects are not linear. They are about relationships between ideas.

Mind maps help you connect concepts. You put the main topic in the center, then you branch out into related ideas, examples, and debates.

Mind maps are especially helpful when you are preparing for exams and when you are trying to see how topics connect across a course.

But mind maps are not magic. They are useful only if you can explain the links. Do not draw a pretty map that you cannot explain. Explanation is the test.

A simple card method for deep understanding

Some students struggle because they always reread and never test themselves.

A simple method is to turn key ideas into question-and-answer cards. The card can be physical or digital.

The front asks a question. The back gives a clear answer in your own words.

This method trains memory and understanding. It is also efficient when your time is limited.

If you have weak power or no internet, physical cards work well. You can revise without devices.

Summarizing without copying

A summary is the author's idea in your words, in fewer lines, with the main meaning intact.

Many students think summarizing means shortening by cutting. That is not enough. You must rebuild the idea in your own language.

A good summary does three things.

It captures the main claim.

It captures the key support or logic.

It keeps the meaning accurate.

To practice, read a paragraph, close the book, then write what it said. Then open the book and check. If you missed a key point, correct it. If you added something that is not there, remove it. This is training in honesty.

Paraphrasing without becoming a thief

Paraphrasing is restating a specific point in your own words, often at the same length.

Bad paraphrasing happens when students replace a few words and keep the same sentence shape. That is not your writing. That is a disguised copy.

Good paraphrasing changes the sentence shape, changes the phrasing, and keeps the meaning.

But even with good paraphrasing, you still cite the source. Citing is not only for direct quotes. It is for ideas that are not yours.

One truth you must accept early is this. Academic integrity is not only about avoiding punishment. It is about building a name you can live with. If your work is built on quiet stealing, your confidence will always be fake. Real confidence comes from real work.

Quotations: when to use them, and when not to

Quotations are useful when the author's wording is special, when a definition must be exact, or when you want to show that a respected voice said something clearly.

Quotations are not useful when they replace your thinking.

A paper full of quotations is usually a paper with a weak writer behind it. A strong paper uses quotations sparingly and explains them well.

When you quote, you must introduce the quote, present the quote, then explain the quote. Many students forget the explanation. They drop a quote and move on. That makes the quote feel like a decoration.

Also, never quote something you do not understand. If you cannot explain it, do not quote it.

Building a personal knowledge bank

A knowledge bank is where your learning accumulates across weeks and across semesters.

Many students study for one exam, then forget everything, then start again from zero next semester. That is a waste.

A knowledge bank can be simple. It can be a notebook, folders of summaries, or a digital note tool. The goal is to store what you learned in a way you can retrieve.

A useful bank has a few features.

It has clear titles.

It has your own summaries, not only copied content.

It has key terms and examples.

It has links between ideas, so you can see how one topic connects to another.

When you build this, writing becomes easier because you already have usable material. Research becomes easier because you already know the key debates. Exams become easier because you are revising, not learning from scratch.

Reading schedules that protect your life

Many students destroy themselves by reading for long hours without a plan. They read until they hate the course. Then they procrastinate. Then they panic.

A better approach is to read in blocks.

A reading block can be thirty minutes, forty-five minutes, or one hour. Inside that block, you read with a purpose and take short notes. Then you stop. You stand up. You rest your eyes. Then you return.

If you live in a place where power and internet are unstable, your reading blocks should match reality. When you have a few hours of power, do not fill it with endless reading. Mix tasks. Download what you need, then read offline, then write notes, then draft. This gives you progress in multiple areas.

I used this approach when life conditions were not friendly. If you wait for a perfect study environment, you may never study. But if you plan around your real environment, you can still grow.

Reading in a second language

Many students study in a language that is not their first language. That adds weight.

If that is you, do not be ashamed. Your brain is doing double work. It is translating while also learning.

To improve, read consistently and write consistently. Reading alone helps, but writing forces deeper learning. Also build a course vocabulary list and revise it weekly.

If you struggle with one paragraph, do not keep rereading it ten times in anger. Read it twice, then write what you think it means. Then check again. That turns confusion into progress.

Also do not isolate yourself. Discuss with classmates. Ask questions in tutorials. Many students silently struggle because they fear embarrassment. But embarrassment is cheaper than failure.

How to know you understood what you read
The test of understanding is explanation.

If you can explain the idea in simple words without looking, you understood it.

If you can give an example, you understood it better.

If you can connect it to another idea, you understood it deeply.

If you cannot explain it, you are still at exposure stage.

Do not confuse exposure with understanding. Many students read a chapter and feel familiar with it, then they assume they know it. Familiarity is not knowledge.

A simple practice is to close the book and write a short explanation as if you are teaching someone younger than you. Teaching language reveals whether you truly know.

Reading for writing

When you read for an essay or a paper, read with your future paragraphs in mind.

Ask, "What point can I use this for?"

Ask, "What claim does this support?"

Ask, "What debate does this connect to?"

Write your notes in a way that your future self can use. That means you record author, year, and page for key points. It also means you write short lines about how the source could fit into your argument.

This stops you from reading widely and writing blindly.

Common reading traps and how to avoid them
One trap is worshiping the text. Some students treat the author like a king. They fear disagreeing. But academic life includes critique. Respect is good. Blind submission is not.

Another trap is fighting the text. Some students read with anger and reject everything. That is also childish. Read to understand first, then evaluate.

Another trap is reading too much. Students think more sources always mean a better paper. Not true. A few strong sources used well can beat many sources used poorly.

Another trap is reading without producing. If you read and never write notes, summaries, or questions, you will forget.

Another trap is reading at the wrong time. When your brain is tired, you can still do lighter tasks such as organizing notes, rewriting summaries, or preparing questions for class. Save heavy close reading for when your mind is fresh.

A final word on reading and dignity

Academic reading can humble you. Sometimes you will feel slow. Sometimes you will feel behind. Sometimes you will feel like others understand faster.

Do not let that become self-hate.

Reading is a long road. The student who wins is the one who stays on the road. Not because they are always strong, but because they return.

If you build the habits in this part, you will notice a change. Your reading speed will improve, your understanding will sharpen, and your writing will become clearer because you will finally have something solid to say.

In the next part, we turn your reading into writing, and we build the habits that protect your voice while still respecting sources.

PART FOUR

Academic Writing Foundations

Academic writing is not a gift some students are born with. It is trained work. It is a set of repeatable actions that produce clear, credible, well-structured papers.

Many students fear writing because they treat it like a talent test. They sit down, stare at the page, and wait for a perfect opening sentence. Nothing comes. Then they panic, rush, and submit something that sounds uncertain and scattered. When the grade comes back low, they conclude, "I am not good at writing."

That conclusion is usually wrong.

Most weak academic writing is not weak because the student is unintelligent. It is weak because the student did not follow a writing process that matches how academic papers are assessed.

This part gives you that process.

I am not teaching "beautiful English." I am teaching writing that earns marks because it answers the question, follows academic standards, uses evidence correctly, and communicates with clarity.

If you can write in this way, you will perform well even when you are studying in imperfect conditions. I have written and studied under unstable power, expensive mobile data, and noisy environments. Those limits did not destroy the work. Lack of method destroys the work. A method protects you.

1. What makes writing "academic"

Academic writing is not about sounding complicated. It is about being trustworthy.

A paper becomes academic when it shows these qualities:

Clarity

The reader understands what you mean without guessing. Your sentences carry one idea at a time. Your paragraphs stay focused.

Structure

Your writing follows a logical order. Your reader can track your argument from start to finish.

Evidence

You do not expect the reader to accept your claims because you are confident. You support claims using credible sources, data, or clearly explained reasoning.

Accuracy

You represent sources correctly. You do not twist what authors said. You do not "decorate" your work with quotes you do not understand.

Accountability

You cite sources properly. You follow instructions. You respect the rubric.

If you aim for these five qualities, your writing improves fast.

2. Writing begins before writing

Most students begin writing at the wrong place. They begin with the introduction.

That is like trying to build the roof before building the walls.

A better order is:

1. Understand the question
2. Build your answer
3. Plan the structure
4. Gather and assign evidence
5. Draft body paragraphs
6. Draft introduction and conclusion
7. Revise and polish

When you follow this order, writing becomes a controlled task, not a mystery.

3. Understanding the assignment question

Many papers fail because the student did not answer the question they were given. They answered a question they preferred.

Before you write one paragraph, do this.

Step A: Rewrite the question in your own words

If you cannot rewrite it, you do not understand it yet.

Step B: Identify the action word

Common action words include:

Describe
Explain
Compare
Analyze
Evaluate
Discuss
Critique
Argue

These words are instructions. They tell you what kind of thinking the marker wants to see.

If you "describe" when the question asked you to "evaluate," you will lose marks even if your writing is fluent.

Step C: Identify the limits

Look for limits such as:

A time period
A location
A specific theory
A certain number of sources
A case study requirement
A word count

Limits are not obstacles. Limits are the shape of the assignment.

Step D: Identify what counts as evidence for this course

Different courses value different kinds of evidence.

Some courses want scholarly journal articles.
Some accept reports from respected organizations.
Some value primary sources.
Some require theory.

Learn what your course values, then write accordingly.

4. The thesis statement

A thesis statement is your main answer in one or two sentences.

It is not your topic.
It is not your intention.
It is not a vague announcement.

Weak thesis: "This paper will discuss corruption."
Weak thesis: "Corruption is bad and must stop."
Weak thesis: "There are many factors that cause corruption."

Stronger thesis: "Public procurement corruption increases when oversight is weak, reporting channels are unsafe, and penalties are inconsistent. Reducing it requires transparent tender processes, independent audits, and enforceable sanctions."

A good thesis does three things:

1. It states your main claim.
2. It hints at your main reasons.
3. It stays specific enough to guide your structure.

Your thesis is your steering wheel. Without it, your paper drifts.

5. Argument vs description

Many students write descriptive papers when the assignment demands an argument.

Description answers: What is it? What happened?
Argument answers: What does it mean? Why does it matter? What should we conclude?

You can use description, but you must not stop there.

A useful habit is to ask yourself after each paragraph:

So what?

If you cannot answer that question, your writing is likely too descriptive.

Another habit is to use "because" language in your planning:

I claim X because A, B, and C.

That simple sentence creates an argument shape.

6. Planning your structure

A strong structure is not decoration. It is how you earn marks.

Most academic papers follow a simple pattern:

Introduction
Body (organized into sections)
Conclusion
References

But inside that pattern, your job is to arrange points in a logical order.

A practical planning method

Before drafting, create a short outline like this:

1. **Main point one**
   Evidence you will use
   How this supports the thesis
2. **Main point two**
   Evidence you will use
   How this supports the thesis
3. **Main point three**
   Evidence you will use
   How this supports the thesis

When your outline connects points to evidence, drafting becomes far easier.

If a point has no evidence, you either need to find support or remove the point.

This protects you from writing "empty paragraphs" that sound confident but prove nothing.

7. Paragraph craft

A paragraph is not a random block of sentences. It is a unit of meaning.

A strong academic paragraph usually contains:

1. A clear point
2. Evidence or example
3. Explanation of the evidence
4. Link back to the thesis and forward to the next point

A simple paragraph formula that works

You can train your writing using this formula:

Point
Evidence
Explain
Link

Here is what it looks like in practice.

Point: State the claim of the paragraph.
Evidence: Provide a source or example.
Explain: Show how the evidence supports your claim.
Link: Connect to your thesis or next paragraph.

Many students stop after evidence. They drop a quote and move on. The marker then asks, "Why is this here?"

Your explanation is where your thinking shows.

8. Cohesion and flow

Markers love writing that is easy to follow.

Your job is not to impress. Your job is to guide the reader.

You create cohesion by:

Using consistent key terms

If you keep changing the key term, you confuse your reader. Choose a term and stick to it.

Using clear transitions

Transitions do not need to be fancy. They need to be honest.

Examples:

This suggests that...
However, this view has limits because...
In contrast, other studies argue that...
A key implication is...
This evidence supports the claim that...

Keeping your paragraphs in logical order

Put the strongest foundation first. Then build.

A common mistake is jumping between ideas as they come to your mind. That feels natural to the writer but confusing to the reader.

Plan first. Then draft.

9. Using evidence without losing your voice

Academic writing is not a collage of other people's words. It is your argument supported by other people's work.

You keep your voice by doing three things.

Lead with your claim, not with the author

Weak: "Smith (2020) says…"
Better: "Reliable feedback improves student performance when it is specific and timely."

Then you cite Smith as support.

This keeps your paper centered on your thinking rather than on the author parade.

Use evidence as support, not as replacement

Evidence exists to strengthen your claim, not to do your thinking for you.

If your paragraph is mostly quotations, your voice disappears.

Explain evidence clearly

Never assume a quote is self-explanatory. After evidence, write:

What it means.
Why it matters.
How it connects to your thesis.

That is academic writing.

10. Quotations, paraphrasing, and summary

When to quote

Quote when:

The wording is especially precise
A definition must remain exact
A line is famous or heavily debated
You need to show the author's exact phrasing

Even then, keep quotes short and purposeful.

How to quote well

A quote needs three parts:

Introduce it
Give the quote
Explain it

If you skip the explanation, the quote is a dead weight.

Paraphrasing

Paraphrasing means restating an idea in your own words. You must still cite the source.

Good paraphrasing changes sentence structure and wording while keeping meaning accurate.

Bad paraphrasing is word replacement while keeping the same sentence shape. That is still too close.

Summary

Summary compresses a larger section into a shorter explanation.

A good summary captures:

The main claim
The main support
The meaning relevant to your paper

Then you connect it to your argument.

11. Avoiding patchwriting and accidental plagiarism

Many students commit plagiarism accidentally because they draft too close to the source.

Here is the safest method.

1. Read the source section.
2. Close the source.
3. Write the idea from memory in your own words.
4. Open the source and check accuracy.
5. Add citation.

This method protects your dignity and your grade.

Also, do not delay citation until the end. Add citations while drafting. If you delay, you will forget what came from where.

12. Building an introduction that works

A good introduction usually contains:

1. The topic and why it matters
2. The specific focus of the paper
3. The thesis statement
4. A brief map of the main points

Do not make your introduction long. It is a doorway, not the whole house.

A common student mistake is writing a long general introduction that uses many words and says little. Markers want you to get to the point.

You can write the introduction last, after you know what your paper truly argues.

That is not cheating. That is good method.

13. Writing conclusions that earn marks

A conclusion is not a place for new evidence.

A strong conclusion does three things:

1. Restates the thesis in fresh words
2. Summarizes the main points briefly
3. Shows the implication or final answer

Avoid ending with vague lines like "more research is needed" unless you explain what kind of research and why.

A conclusion should leave the marker thinking, "This student answered the question clearly."

14. Drafting under pressure without destroying quality

Many students write under pressure because they started late. If that happens, you must still protect quality.

Here is what to do.

Draft the body first

Write your strongest points first. Do not waste time searching for a perfect opening sentence.

Use placeholders

If you cannot remember a reference detail, write a placeholder like:

[Citation needed]
[Author, year]
[Page number]

Then fix it during revision.

This prevents the common trap of stopping the whole draft because one detail is missing.

Keep moving

The first draft exists to get ideas onto the page. Clarity comes in revision.

15. Revision: where grades are won

Many students submit first drafts. That is why they stay at average grades.

Revision is not "checking grammar." Revision is improving thinking and structure.

A strong revision process has levels.

Level 1: Answer check

Are you answering the exact question?
Did you follow the action word?
Did you meet the source requirements?

Level 2: Argument check

Is your thesis clear?
Do your points logically support the thesis?
Do you have any paragraphs that do not belong?

Level 3: Evidence check

Does each key claim have support?
Are you using credible sources?
Did you explain evidence, not only insert it?

Level 4: Paragraph check

Does each paragraph have one point?
Do paragraphs flow logically?
Do topic sentences guide the reader?

Level 5: Sentence and style check

Are sentences clear and direct?
Did you remove repetition?
Did you keep your terms consistent?

Level 6: Reference check

Are citations complete and consistent?
Does every in-text citation appear in the reference list?
Does every reference list entry appear in the paper?

If you follow these levels, your work improves quickly.

When my environment made study time rare, revision became even more important. If you only have a few hours of power and a limited window to submit, you cannot rely on luck. You must rely on process. Draft offline, revise offline, then use internet time only for uploading and final checks.

16. Editing and proofreading

Editing and proofreading are not the same.

Editing improves clarity and style.
Proofreading catches small errors.

Proofreading should be the last step, after revision.

A simple proofreading method:

1. Read the paper out loud. You will hear awkward sentences.
2. Read it slowly from the end to the beginning for grammar and spelling. This breaks your familiarity and helps you catch errors.
3. Check formatting and headings.
4. Check citations and references.

If you have time, proofread in two sessions with a break between them. Fresh eyes catch more.

17. Academic tone without sounding unnatural

Academic tone is not about sounding like a machine. It is about sounding serious, careful, and clear.

A good tone avoids:

Emotional exaggeration
Personal attacks
Unsupported sweeping claims
Overconfident language without evidence

A good tone uses:

Clear claims
Careful wording when evidence is limited
Precise terms
Respect for sources and opposing views

You can still write with strength. Strength comes from evidence and clarity, not from aggressive language.

18. Common writing problems and fixes

Problem: "My writing is too general."

Fix: Narrow your thesis and use specific evidence.

Problem: "My paragraphs are long and confusing."

Fix: One paragraph, one point. Split large paragraphs.

Problem: "My lecturer says I am descriptive."

Fix: Add analysis. After describing evidence, explain why it matters for your argument.

Problem: "I do not know how to start."

Fix: Start with the body. Start with one paragraph you can write today.

Problem: "I lose marks on referencing."

Fix: Track sources from day one. Add citations while drafting. Do not rely on memory.

19. A writing routine that survives real life

Many books assume you have a calm desk every day. Many students do not.

If your life includes unstable power, weak internet, family demands, or work responsibilities, your writing routine must match reality.

Here is a routine that works even in difficult conditions.

1. Keep one "assignment file" where everything lives. Notes, outline, draft, sources.
2. Draft offline whenever possible.
3. Do internet tasks in batches: download, email, submit, back up.
4. Use short writing blocks consistently. Even 30 minutes can move a paper forward.
5. End each block by writing the next sentence you will write tomorrow. This reduces friction when you return.

This is how you build progress without waiting for perfect conditions.

20. Practice section: build one strong paragraph today

Choose a claim related to one of your courses.

Write:

1. A topic sentence stating the claim
2. One piece of evidence from a credible source
3. Two to four sentences explaining the evidence
4. One link sentence connecting back to your thesis

Do this exercise often. Paragraph training is writing strength training.

Closing note for Part Four

If you understand the question, build a clear thesis, plan your structure, write focused paragraphs, use evidence properly, and revise in layers, your writing will improve dramatically.

This is not theory. It is method.

Next we move into Part Five, where we apply these foundations to the common assignments students meet, from essays and reports to proposals, presentations, and group work.

PART FIVE
Common Academic Assignments

A student can understand the theory of academic writing and still struggle the moment a real assignment appears. That is because assignments come in different shapes, and each shape has its own rules.

If you treat every assignment like the same thing, you will keep losing marks. You will write an essay when the task was a report. You will tell a story when the task demanded analysis. You will use sources like decoration when the task demanded evaluation. Then you will say, "But I wrote many pages."

In university, pages do not win marks. Accuracy wins marks.

This part teaches you the common assignment types you will meet, what lecturers usually expect from them, and how to approach each one with a method that works in real life.

I also want to say something direct. Many students fear assignments because they wait until pressure week. Then every assignment feels like a monster. If you start earlier and work in small blocks, the monster becomes normal work. Even with unstable power and expensive internet, early work gives you space. Late work steals your space.

Short responses and reflection papers

Short responses look easy, but they are where many students lose marks because they become casual. A short response still needs focus, still needs evidence when required, and still needs structure.

What lecturers usually want

Lecturers often use short responses to test whether you read and understood. They want to see:

- A direct answer to the prompt
- One or two key ideas from the reading or lecture
- A clear example or evidence
- Your brief evaluation or connection to the course theme

How to structure a strong short response

A reliable structure is:

- One sentence that answers the question
- A short explanation of why that answer makes sense
- One piece of supporting evidence or example
- One closing line that links to a bigger idea from the course

Reflection papers without turning them into diaries

A reflection paper is not a diary entry. It can include personal experience, but it must still show thinking.

A lecturer usually expects:

- What you learned
- Why it matters
- How it connects to the reading, lecture, or practice
- What changed in your thinking, if anything

A strong reflection uses "I" carefully. Not "I feel" without support, but "I noticed," "I realized," "I struggled with," followed by explanation and connection to course ideas.

Common mistakes

- Summarizing the reading without answering the prompt
- Writing feelings without linking to course concepts
- Writing general statements like "This is important" without explaining why

Essays

The essay is one of the most common assignments. Many students think essays are just long writing. In reality, essays are structured arguments.

What lecturers usually want

- A clear thesis that answers the question
- A logical structure of points that support the thesis
- Use of scholarly sources
- Analysis, not only description
- Correct referencing and formatting

Planning an essay that does not collapse

Before you write, build these items:

- Your rewritten assignment question
- The action word and what it demands
- Your thesis statement
- Your main points, each linked to evidence

A simple way to test your plan is to say your thesis out loud, then list your three main reasons. If you cannot do that, your plan is still weak.

Essay structure that works in most courses

Introduction:

- Topic and focus
- Thesis statement
- Brief map of main points

Body:

- Point, evidence, explanation, link
- Repeat with logical order

Conclusion:

- Restate thesis in fresh words
- Summarize main points
- State the final implication or answer

Strong essays use a balance of sources

A common student error is using one source heavily and a few sources lightly. A stronger approach is to use sources across your points, so your argument looks supported from multiple angles.

When an essay becomes weak

- When paragraphs do not connect to the thesis
- When the essay is a list of facts instead of a line of reasoning
- When quotations replace explanation
- When the student argues with emotion instead of evidence

Research papers

A research paper is more than an essay. It usually demands deeper engagement with sources and a clearer demonstration of inquiry.

Many students fear research papers because they assume they must discover something new like a scientist. In undergraduate work, "research" usually means you are building a strong answer using scholarly evidence, not inventing a new theory.

What lecturers usually want

- A focused research question
- Evidence-based argument
- A clear use of academic sources
- Strong organization
- Good method of handling literature, even if it is small

What makes a research paper different from a normal essay

- The question tends to be more specific

- The paper may include a short background section
- The paper usually engages more directly with scholarly debate
- The paper may require a clearer explanation of how sources were selected and used

A practical structure for many research papers

Introduction:

- Problem and importance
- Research question
- Thesis or central claim
- Brief plan of the paper

Background or key concepts:

- Definitions and key ideas needed

Main sections:

- Themes, debates, or arguments supported by sources

Conclusion:

- Clear answer to the research question
- Limitations or scope boundaries, stated honestly
- Implications or recommendation if appropriate

A word about limited internet and research papers

If your internet is expensive or unstable, treat research like a harvest.

When you have connection, search and download in one focused session. Save PDFs. Save citation details. Save your source notes. Then work offline for days if needed. This method protects you from losing momentum.

I used this approach often. When mobile data finished too quickly, the only way to keep writing was to prepare offline work that did not depend on connection.

Literature reviews

A literature review can be a full assignment or a section inside a larger paper. Students struggle with it because they think it is summary. It is not.

A literature review is organized reading. It shows what scholars have said, where they agree, where they disagree, and what gaps remain.

What lecturers usually want

- The major themes in the literature
- Evidence that you read credible sources, not random websites
- A logical organization, not a list
- A clear conclusion about what the literature shows overall

How to organize a literature review

You can organize by:

Themes:

- Studies focusing on one factor

- Studies focusing on another factor

Time:

- Earlier work vs newer work

Method:

- Qualitative vs quantitative studies

Debate:

- One school of thought vs another

What not to do

- "Author A says this. Author B says that." repeated for ten paragraphs
- A literature review that never forms a conclusion about the overall direction
- Ignoring disagreements and pretending all sources say the same thing

The simplest way to write it

Start by grouping your sources into themes. Then write theme by theme.

Inside each theme:

- Summarize the main idea
- Compare sources briefly
- Point out limits
- Link to your research focus

When done well, a literature review makes the rest of your writing easier because it builds your foundation.

Reports

Reports are common in business, development studies, public health, engineering, and many applied fields. Students often write reports like essays and lose marks.

A report is not an essay. A report is structured for fast understanding and practical decision-making.

What lecturers usually want

- Clear headings and sections
- Direct presentation of findings or information
- Use of data or evidence
- Practical recommendations when appropriate
- Professional formatting

Typical report sections

Depending on the course, a report may include:

- Title page
- Executive summary
- Introduction and purpose
- Background
- Method or approach (sometimes brief)
- Findings
- Discussion
- Recommendations
- Conclusion

- References
- Appendices (tables, tools, extra material)

What makes a report strong

- The reader can skim and still understand
- Headings match the task and the rubric
- Findings are separated from opinions
- Recommendations are based on evidence, not personal preference

Common mistakes

- Writing long paragraphs with no headings
- Mixing findings and recommendations without explaining the connection
- Hiding key results in the middle of the report instead of presenting them clearly

Case studies

Case studies are common in law, business, public administration, health, and social sciences. A case study asks you to analyze a specific situation using course concepts.

What lecturers usually want

- Clear description of the case facts (brief but accurate)
- Identification of the main issue or problem
- Application of relevant theory or concepts
- Evaluation of options

- A justified recommendation or conclusion

A practical case study structure

- Case summary: what happened
- Key issue: what matters most
- Analysis: apply concepts or models
- Options: possible actions or interpretations
- Recommendation: best option and why
- Implementation or implications: what it would require

Common mistakes

- Retelling the case like a story and forgetting analysis
- Offering recommendations without criteria
- Ignoring constraints inside the case, like budget, time, ethics, or policy limits

A strong case study feels like careful thinking under real conditions.

Lab reports

Lab reports are common in sciences and health fields, and they have a very specific structure. Students lose marks when they write lab reports like essays.

What lecturers usually want

- Clear method and accurate reporting
- Results presented correctly, often with tables or graphs

- Discussion that interprets results and addresses error sources
- Proper scientific tone and referencing when needed

Common lab report sections

- Title
- Aim or objective
- Introduction (brief theory background)
- Method
- Results
- Discussion
- Conclusion
- References (if required)

The biggest mistake in lab reports

The biggest mistake is mixing results and discussion. Results are what you observed. Discussion is what it means.

Also, never hide errors. Good lab work acknowledges errors and explains how they may have affected results.

Proposals and concept notes

A proposal asks you to plan a project or a research activity. It is not the final work. It is a plan that must convince someone that your project is clear, meaningful, and doable.

What lecturers usually want

- A clear problem statement
- A focused objective or research question

- A workable plan or method
- A realistic timeline
- A brief explanation of expected outcomes

Typical proposal sections

For research:

- Title
- Background and problem statement
- Objectives or research questions
- Brief literature basis
- Method
- Ethical considerations (when relevant)
- Timeline
- References

For projects or development:

- Background and problem
- Goal and objectives
- Activities
- Target group
- Risks and mitigation
- Budget summary (sometimes)
- Monitoring and evaluation idea
- Timeline

How to write proposals that are not fantasies

Many proposals fail because they promise too much. A strong proposal respects limits.

A good test is this:
If you had to do this project with your current time, tools, and conditions, could you do it?

If the answer is no, scale it down.

In difficult environments, realism is not weakness. It is maturity.

Presentations and posters

Many courses require presentations. Students often fear presentations more than essays because presentations expose you in public. The truth is that presentations are also a skill, and they can be trained.

What lecturers usually want

- Clear structure and timing
- A strong central message
- Evidence-based points
- Professional delivery
- Slides that support you, not replace you

A simple presentation structure

- Opening: topic and why it matters
- Main message: your thesis or key claim
- Two or three supporting points with evidence
- Brief conclusion: what the audience should remember
- Questions

Slides: what students get wrong

Students write too many words on slides. Then they read slides. That makes the audience bored and makes you look unprepared.

A better approach:

- Use slides for headings, key terms, and simple visuals
- Speak the explanation, do not paste it on the slide

Posters

Posters are designed for visual scanning. They are not mini essays.

A good poster has:

- Clear title
- Brief background
- Method or approach
- Key findings
- Simple visuals
- Short conclusion and implication
- References if required

Group projects

Group projects are where many students learn painful lessons. Group work can be powerful, but it can also become conflict and frustration when no system exists.

What lecturers usually want

- Evidence of collaboration
- Quality work as a group product
- Clear division of roles
- Professional presentation or report

Why group projects fail

- No clear roles
- No timeline
- No agreed quality standard
- One person carries the load
- Conflict avoided until late

A simple group system that prevents chaos

At the start, agree on:

- Roles: leader, researcher, writer, editor, presenter, data handler
- Deadlines: internal deadlines earlier than the official deadline
- Tools: one shared folder, one document version rule
- Quality standard: follow the rubric
- Meeting schedule: short and regular

Also agree on one rule:

Nobody submits anything without review by at least one other person.

Handling conflict without destroying the work

If someone is not working, do not gossip. Communicate early, clearly, and politely.

If the problem continues, document your communication. Many courses allow reporting non-participation, but you must show evidence.

A group project is still an academic task, not a friendship test. Handle it with maturity.

One method to approach any assignment

No matter the assignment type, you can protect yourself with the same basic method.

- Understand the action word and the rubric
- Rewrite the task in your own words
- Plan structure before drafting
- Assign sources or evidence to points
- Draft body first
- Revise in layers
- Check formatting and references

Students who do this consistently stop feeling confused. They start feeling in control.

A quick assignment selection guide

When you are not sure what you are writing, ask:

If the goal is to argue a position using sources, it is likely an essay.

If the goal is to present findings, options, and recommendations for action, it is likely a report.

If the goal is to analyze one situation using concepts, it is likely a case study.

If the goal is to plan research or a project, it is likely a proposal.

If the goal is to describe method, results, and interpretation, it is likely a lab report.

If the goal is to map scholarly debate, it is likely a literature review.

If you identify the type early, you avoid writing in the wrong shape.

Closing note for Part Five

Many students suffer because they treat assignments like surprises. But assignments are patterns. Once you learn the patterns, you can prepare early and work steadily.

In the next part, we will focus on referencing and academic integrity. That is where many good students lose marks, not because they are dishonest, but because they are careless or untrained. We will fix that with simple, reliable habits.

PART SIX
Referencing and Academic Integrity

Referencing is not a punishment. It is proof that you did real work.

When you reference well, you show three things at once.

First, you show respect for other people's ideas. Second, you show that your claims have support. Third, you show that your paper can be checked.

That last point matters more than many students realize. In academic life, trust is built through traceability. A reader should be able to ask, "Where did this come from?" and your paper should answer clearly.

Many students lose marks here, not because they are dishonest, but because they are untrained or careless. Others fall into plagiarism because they panic near deadlines and start copying without thinking. Both problems can be fixed with method.

This part gives you that method.

Why citation matters

A university paper is part of a long human conversation. People have been asking questions, testing ideas, arguing, correcting, and building knowledge long before you arrived. Referencing is how you join that conversation without pretending you invented everything.

When you cite sources, you are saying:

- This idea came from here.
- This evidence was found by these authors.
- This definition is not mine.
- This claim is supported by this study.

Your lecturer can then judge your work fairly, because they can see:

- What you contributed
- What you borrowed
- How strong your supporting sources are
- Whether you used sources accurately

Without citation, even a well-written paper becomes suspicious. The marker cannot tell what is yours and what is not.

Academic integrity as personal dignity

Academic integrity is often taught as fear: "Do not plagiarize or you will be punished."

That message is true, but it is too small.

Integrity means you can stand behind your work without shame. It means your grades are not built on quiet theft. It means your confidence is real because your effort is real.

When students cheat, they usually do it for one of these reasons:

- They started late and panicked.

- They did not understand the assignment.
- They did not know how to paraphrase.
- They did not know how to cite.

They feared failure more than they respected themselves.

If you build a system early, you reduce panic. When panic reduces, cheating temptation reduces.

What counts as plagiarism

Plagiarism is presenting someone else's work as yours. It can happen in obvious and subtle ways.

It includes:

- Copying sentences without quotation marks and citation
- Copying paragraphs and changing a few words
- Paraphrasing an idea but failing to cite the source
- Using a unique structure or sequence of ideas from a source and presenting it as your own plan
- Submitting another student's work
- Paying someone to write for you
- Reusing your own previous work in a new course without permission, if your school treats that as misconduct

Many students think plagiarism only means copy-paste. That is the loud version. The quiet version is when your writing stays too close to the original source in sentence shape and vocabulary.

The marker may still treat it as plagiarism because your writing does not show independent expression.

Common risk areas

Some parts of student work carry higher risk.

- Paraphrasing technical material
- Writing literature reviews
- Writing background sections that summarize many sources
- Using AI tools to rewrite source material
- Rushing near the deadline
- Taking notes by copying, then forgetting to rewrite in your own words later

If you recognize these risk areas early, you can protect yourself with better habits.

The difference between quoting, paraphrasing, and summarizing

These are not the same. Students often mix them and create problems.

Quoting

You use the author's exact words.
You place them in quotation marks (or block quote format if the quote is long, depending on the style guide).
You cite the source with page number when required.

Use quoting when wording matters, such as:

- Exact definitions

- Key statements where phrasing is important
- Short lines you plan to analyze closely

Quoting too much is weak writing. It makes your paper feel borrowed.

Paraphrasing

You restate a specific idea from a source in your own words, usually at similar length.

You still cite the source.

Paraphrasing shows understanding. It keeps your voice in control.

Summarizing

You compress a larger section into a shorter explanation in your own words.

You still cite the source.

Summary is useful for showing the overall direction of a source, especially in literature reviews.

A simple rule:

If the idea is not yours, citation is required, whether you quote, paraphrase, or summarize.

Patchwriting and how to avoid it

Patchwriting is when you change a few words but keep the same sentence shape and flow from the source. It often happens when students draft while looking at the source. Their eyes copy the structure even if they change words.

The safest method is this:

- Read the source section.
- Close it.
- Write the idea from memory in your own words.
- Open the source again to check accuracy.
- Add your citation.

This method protects you from accidental copying, and it strengthens your learning.

In-text citations and reference lists

Most styles have two main parts:

In-text citations appear inside your paragraphs. They show where a claim came from.

The reference list appears at the end. It shows full details so the reader can find the source.

If one part is missing, your referencing is incomplete.

A practical way to think of it:

- In-text citation = quick direction
- Reference entry = full address

The three common systems: APA, MLA, Chicago

Different fields prefer different styles. Your course outline usually tells you which one to use.

APA

Common in social sciences, education, psychology, health, business, and many other fields.

Often uses author and year in-text.

Example shape: (Author, Year)

MLA

Common in literature, language studies, and many humanities subjects.

Often uses author and page number in-text.

Example shape: (Author Page)

Chicago

Common in history and some humanities. Can be used with footnotes or with author-date format depending on the course.

The key lesson is simple. Do not mix styles. Pick the style your lecturer demands and follow it consistently.

How to cite ideas correctly in your writing

Many students believe citation only belongs at the end of a paragraph. That can be risky, because the marker may not know which sentence the citation supports.

A safer practice is to cite close to the idea you borrowed.

- If one sentence uses a source, cite that sentence.

- If a whole paragraph is built from one source, you can cite early and again when needed, especially after key claims.

Also, learn to cite without breaking your flow.

You can use "author as part of the sentence" when it reads naturally:

Some studies argue that feedback works best when it is specific and timely (Author, Year).
Author (Year) explains that…

Both are fine. What matters is clarity and consistency.

Page numbers and when they matter

Rules differ across styles and courses, but these habits are safe in most cases.

- Use page numbers for direct quotations.
- Use page numbers when you paraphrase a very specific point from a page, especially in APA if your course encourages it.
- Use page numbers when you cite a definition pulled from a specific line.

For general paraphrasing of a whole article's findings, page numbers may not always be required, but adding them can strengthen accuracy if your course allows it.

Secondary citation and why it is risky

Secondary citation is when you quote or cite something that you did not read directly, but you found it inside another author's work.

Example: You did not read Author A, but you read Author B who quoted Author A.

This is risky because:

- You might misrepresent Author A.
- Author B might have quoted selectively.
- You might miss important details.

Best habit: read the original source if possible.

If you cannot access the original, your course may allow secondary citation. If allowed, be honest about it and follow the style guide rule. Do not pretend you read what you did not read.

Managing your sources from day one

Most referencing problems begin early, not at the end.

Students read sources, take notes, then later forget where ideas came from. Near submission day, they try to rebuild references from memory. That is where errors multiply.

The simplest fix is a source record system.

Create one "Sources" page for every assignment. For each source, record:

Author(s)
Year
Title
Journal or publisher
Where you found it (database name or URL saved
privately)
Page numbers for key points you may use

Then, when you take notes, link your notes to that source.

If your internet is unstable or expensive, this habit matters
even more. When you finally have connection, you may
not have time to hunt again for the same article. A clean
source record protects your work.

I used this approach because there were days when the
internet disappeared with the generator, and days when
mobile data finished too quickly. If I did not save PDFs
and citation details early, the work would have collapsed
later.

Reference list accuracy: the quiet mark-winner

Markers notice reference lists.

A strong reference list communicates seriousness. A weak
one communicates carelessness, even if your argument is
good.

Common reference list problems include:

- Missing sources that were cited in the text
- Sources listed that never appear in the text
- Inconsistent capitalization

- Wrong italics usage
- Missing volume, issue, or page range for articles
- Broken formatting across entries

A quick discipline that protects you:

- After drafting, do a citation audit.
- Go through your paper and list every in-text citation.
- Then compare it to your reference list.
- Every in-text citation must have a matching reference entry.
- Every reference entry must be used in the paper.

This one check can lift your grade.

Quoting correctly without damaging your paper

A quote should not appear like a sudden foreign object inside your paragraph. It needs a home.

A reliable method:

- Introduce the quote with your own claim.
- Present the quote.
- Explain it in your own words.
- Connect it back to your thesis.

Also keep quotes short.

Short quotes are easier to explain and easier to integrate. Long quotes often signal that the student did not want to write their own explanation.

If your style guide uses block quotes for long quotations, use them only when required, and always explain them afterward.

Paraphrasing with integrity

The goal of paraphrasing is not to hide copying. The goal is to express understanding while keeping meaning accurate.

A strong paraphrase does two things:

1. It changes the wording and sentence shape.
2. It keeps the meaning intact.

If you change meaning, you misrepresent the source. That is also a form of academic dishonesty, even if you cited it, because you are using the author to support a claim they did not make.

A simple accuracy test:

After paraphrasing, compare your paraphrase to the source and ask:

- Did I keep the meaning?
- Did I remove important conditions or limits?
- Did I add claims not present?
- Did I make it sound stronger or weaker than the author intended?

Accuracy is part of integrity.

Using citation tools without becoming lazy

Citation tools can help you move faster, but they can also produce incorrect references. They often get:

- Capitalization wrong
- Missing authors wrong
- Publisher details incomplete
- Page ranges missing
- Website dates confusing

If you use a tool, still check the output. Your name is on the paper, not the tool's name.

Also, do not use a tool as your source record. Keep your own list anyway. Tools fail, phones break, accounts log out, power goes off. A simple source list in your assignment folder survives.

Using AI tools responsibly

Many institutions now have rules about AI use. Some allow it for grammar support, structure checking, or brainstorming. Some restrict it heavily. Your course outline, department rules, and university policy matter.

A safe student rule is this:

- Never use a tool to hide copying.
- Never paste source text into a tool and ask it to rewrite, then submit the output as your own.
- Never ask a tool to write your assignment and submit it as if you authored it.

If your school allows limited support, keep it limited and transparent where required.

Even when allowed, remember this: academic growth comes from doing the thinking yourself. Tools can polish, but they cannot replace your training without stealing your progress.

If you want a clean way to use tools safely, use them after you have drafted, not before. Let them help you with clarity, grammar, and formatting checks, not with replacing your ideas.

Integrity under deadline pressure

Students often break integrity rules when they are under stress. The stress usually came from starting late.

The cure is not only moral advice. The cure is planning.

If you start earlier, you have time to:

- Read properly
- Take clean notes
- Draft in your own words
- Check citations
- Revise calmly

If you start late, you create a situation where shortcuts seem attractive.

So treat time management as part of academic integrity. They are connected.

A student with a steady weekly rhythm is less likely to plagiarize than a student who works only in panic week.

A reference-check routine you can follow every time

Use this routine before submission.

Read the assignment instructions again and confirm required citation style.

- Check that every borrowed idea has an in-text citation.
- Check that every direct quote has quotation marks and page number when required.
- Check that every in-text citation has a matching reference entry.
- Check that every reference entry appears in the paper at least once.
- Check consistency of formatting across reference entries.
- Check spelling of author names and years.
- Check that your sources match the requirement, such as "peer-reviewed sources only" if stated.

This routine sounds simple, but it prevents many avoidable mark losses.

A short warning about "common knowledge"

Students sometimes ask, "Do I need to cite this?"

A safe answer is:

- If it is a widely known fact in the field, it may be treated as common knowledge.
- If it is a specific claim, a statistic, a debated point, a definition from a specific author, or a finding from a study, cite it.
- If you are unsure, cite. It is safer to cite than to guess.

Also, lecturers often prefer more citation than less, as long as citations are relevant and not spam.

Integrity in group work

Group work creates special problems.

One member may copy material from the internet and insert it into the group report. If the report is submitted, the whole group may suffer.

Protect yourself with one group rule:

Nothing enters the final document without review by at least one other member.

Also keep a record of contributions where possible, so responsibility is traceable.

A group project is not only about the final document. It is also about how you work. Professional habits matter.

Closing note for Part Six

Referencing is not an extra task added to hurt students. It is part of what makes academic writing credible.

When you reference well, your work becomes stronger, your thinking becomes cleaner, and your confidence becomes honest.

In the next part, we move into study skills and performance. That is where you learn how to manage time, build routines, prepare for exams, and keep steady progress even when life is not stable.

PART SEVEN

Study Skills, Time Management, and Exam Performance

A student can understand lectures, write good essays, and still fail because their study life is disorganized. That is painful because it feels unfair. You know you can do the work, yet your grades do not reflect your ability.

This part is about fixing that gap.

Study skills are not motivational quotes. They are operating habits. Time management is not about being busy. It is about being intentional. Exam performance is not about luck. It is about preparation and retrieval.

If you build the habits in this part, your academic life becomes calmer. You stop guessing. You stop running on panic. You stop depending on last-minute miracles.

And if your environment is not stable, these skills matter even more. When power can disappear, when internet is expensive, when noise and heat interfere, you cannot afford random methods. You need methods that survive real conditions.

1. The real purpose of time management

Time management is not about squeezing every minute. It is about protecting what matters.

A semester has limited hours. You cannot create more. You can only decide where they go.

Time management gives you:

- Early start advantage
- Less stress near deadlines
- Better sleep before exams
- Higher quality writing through revision time
- Reduced temptation to copy or rush

Many students underestimate revision time. They plan only for drafting. That is why their final work is weak. Drafting creates material. Revision creates quality.

If you schedule revision, your grades rise.

2. The difference between a busy student and an effective student

Busy students do many things. Effective students do the right things.

A busy student spends hours rereading notes without testing understanding.

An effective student reads, then practices recall.

A busy student writes long drafts late.

An effective student drafts early and revises in layers.

A busy student searches for sources every day.

An effective student searches in batches and works offline when needed.

A busy student attends lectures but does not review.

An effective student reviews within 24 hours and turns lecture content into usable notes.

You do not need to be busy. You need to be effective.

3. Building your weekly rhythm

Your weekly rhythm is your academic backbone. Without it, you depend on motivation and panic.

A good rhythm answers:

- When will I read?
- When will I write?
- When will I revise?
- When will I review lecture notes?
- When will I rest?

Here is a practical weekly shape that works for many students:

- Lecture days: attend, take notes, then do a short review that same day
- Two reading blocks per course per week
- Two writing blocks per week, even when no assignment feels urgent
- One weekly review block where you consolidate notes and check deadlines

If your week is full, shorten blocks. Do not remove them.

A 30-minute block done consistently is more powerful than a 5-hour block done once.

4. Two rhythms for unstable power and internet

Many study guides ignore this reality. But many students live it.

When power and internet are stable, study can be smooth.

When power and internet are unstable, the student must adapt or fall behind.

The most effective method is the two-rhythm system.

Rhythm A: When you have internet and power

Use this time for tasks that require connection:

- Download reading materials
- Save webpages as PDF
- Search for sources
- Access library databases
- Email lecturers
- Upload assignments
- Back up work to cloud or external storage

Do not waste connection time reading long articles online. Download them and read offline.

Rhythm B: When you do not have internet or power

Use this time for offline tasks:

- Read saved PDFs
- Outline assignments
- Draft paragraphs

- Revise and edit drafts
- Create recall notes for exams
- Practice past questions

This method saved me many times. In places where internet depended on a generator, waiting for perfect conditions was a way of losing. Planning for reality was the only way to keep moving.

5. The "semester page" and the "weekly page"

Students fail not because they are weak, but because they cannot see their workload clearly.

Your brain cannot manage what it cannot see.

Use two pages:

The semester page

One page that lists each course and all assessments with dates and weight.

This page is your map.

The weekly page

Each Sunday or Monday, write your plan for the week:

- Reading blocks
- Writing blocks
- Deadlines
- Tutorial preparation
- Small tasks such as printing, formatting, and submission checks

This weekly page turns your semester map into action.

6. Managing multiple courses without mental collapse

When you have several courses, it is easy to feel overwhelmed. Your mind jumps from one deadline to another, and nothing feels finished.

The solution is not "work harder." The solution is controlled rotation.

Controlled rotation method

Each week, you rotate attention across courses using fixed blocks.

Example:

Monday: Course A reading, Course B review
Tuesday: Course C tutorial prep, Course A summary notes
Wednesday: Course B reading, writing block
Thursday: Course C reading, Course D review
Friday: writing block, referencing check
Weekend: consolidation and planning

This method keeps all courses alive. None becomes a surprise disaster.

7. Procrastination: what it really is

Procrastination is not laziness. Many times it is fear wearing normal clothes.

Students procrastinate because:

- They fear not doing it perfectly

- They do not know how to start
- The task feels too big
- They are tired and mentally overloaded
- They are distracted by phones and social media

To defeat procrastination, you do not need extreme discipline. You need a method for starting.

The smallest-action method

Ask:
What is the smallest action that moves this task forward in five minutes?

Examples:

- Open the assignment and rewrite the question
- Write the thesis in one sentence
- Create the outline headings
- Find two sources and save them
- Draft one paragraph

Once you start, momentum often follows.

Use time limits

Give yourself 25 minutes to work, then a short break. This protects attention and reduces fear.

Reduce friction

Make your study space ready. Open your documents. Keep your materials in one place. If starting feels difficult, you will delay.

8. Memory and learning: what actually works

Many students study by rereading and highlighting. That feels productive, but it often creates weak memory.

Learning becomes strong when you practice retrieval, not exposure.

The difference between exposure and retrieval

Exposure is reading and feeling familiar.

Retrieval is forcing your brain to recall without looking.

Exams reward retrieval.

So your study method must train retrieval.

9. Active recall: the core exam skill

Active recall means you test yourself.

You ask questions and try to answer without looking.

This can be done through:

- Practice questions
- Flashcards
- Explaining concepts out loud
- Writing short summaries from memory
- Teaching a peer

A simple rule:
If you only reread, you are studying lightly.
If you recall without looking, you are studying deeply.

10. Spaced repetition: why cramming fails

Cramming feels powerful because it creates short-term familiarity. But it often collapses after the exam.

Spaced repetition means you review material over time, with increasing gaps.

Example:
Review after 1 day
Then after 3 days
Then after 7 days
Then after 14 days

This strengthens memory because the brain learns to retrieve information after forgetting begins.

You do not need fancy apps. You can do this with a calendar and your notes.

11. Note consolidation: turning class notes into exam notes

Class notes are often messy. Exam notes must be clean.

After each lecture, do a quick consolidation within 24 hours:

- Rewrite key ideas in your own words
- Define key terms
- Write one example for each key concept
- Write one possible exam question related to the lecture

This transforms lectures into usable study material.

Students who do this weekly rarely panic near exams because their exam notes are already built.

12. Exam preparation by exam type

Exams are not all the same. Preparation must match the exam format.

Multiple choice exams

These test recognition and detail.

Preparation:

- Practice questions
- Clear definitions
- Distinguish similar terms
- Learn common traps and how questions are framed

Short answer exams

These test recall and clean explanation.

Preparation:

- Practice writing short explanations
- Learn key terms and examples
- Practice answering under time limits

Essay exams

These test argument, structure, and evidence.

Preparation:

- Practice essay plans, not full essays every time
- Build thesis statements quickly
- Prepare examples and key theorists
- Practice writing introductions and conclusions under time limits

Open-book exams

Open-book does not mean easy. It tests your ability to use material quickly.

Preparation:

- Organize notes for fast retrieval
- Create summary sheets
- Mark key page numbers and sections
- Practice using your materials under time

Students fail open-book exams because they think the book will save them. The book does not save unprepared minds.

13. Past papers and practice questions

Past papers are one of the strongest study tools because they show:

- The style of questions
- The depth expected
- The topics repeated
- The marking pattern

If your department provides past papers, use them early, not only in exam week.

A strong approach:

- Start with one past question each week
- Write an outline answer
- Then check your notes and improve
- Later, practice under timed conditions

This turns exam preparation into training, not panic.

14. Writing exams: speed, structure, and calm

Many students know the content but fail because they cannot organize under time pressure.

Train structure under time.

A simple essay exam method

Before writing the essay, spend 5 to 10 minutes planning.

Write:

- Thesis statement
- 3 main points
- Evidence or examples for each
- Conclusion point

Then write.

Students who skip planning often write long, messy answers and lose marks for structure.

15. Managing stress and mental load

Stress is not always bad. A small amount can sharpen focus. But uncontrolled stress ruins memory, ruins sleep, and ruins performance.

A student must manage stress like any other academic skill.

Protect sleep before exams

Sleep affects memory retrieval. A sleepless night can damage recall even if you studied.

Eat and hydrate

This sounds simple, but many students ignore it. Brain performance is physical.

Movement

Short walks can reset the mind. Sitting for 12 hours does not always produce more learning.

Break big tasks into small blocks

Large tasks create fear. Small blocks create progress.

Avoid isolation

Discussing material with classmates can reduce stress and strengthen understanding.

16. Studying in noisy or crowded environments

If you live in a crowded home or noisy area, you may not have silence.

You can still study with strategy:

- Use earplugs or headphones if possible
- Use short blocks when noise is lower (early morning or late evening)
- Use written recall exercises that keep your mind active
- Use offline reading to reduce device distractions

If you only wait for silence, you will study less than you should.

17. The week before exams: what to do and what not to do

What to do

- Review summary notes
- Practice questions
- Identify weak areas and fix them
- Practice timed answers
- Sleep consistently

What not to do

- Start new topics from scratch
- Study all night repeatedly
- Panic and change methods suddenly
- Compare yourself to others until you lose confidence

The week before exams is not the time for chaos. It is the time for focused strengthening.

18. After exams: learning from performance

Many students finish an exam and never reflect. Then they repeat mistakes.

After each exam or major assignment, ask:

- What worked?
- What failed?
- What should I change next time?

Write answers in a small notebook. That notebook becomes your personal academic training manual.

Closing note for Part Seven

Study skills are not separate from academic writing and research. They are what makes those skills usable under real semester pressure.

When you build weekly rhythm, practice recall, and prepare using past questions, exams become predictable, and stress reduces.

Next, we move into communication, campus life, and professional growth: how to work with lecturers, how to use academic support systems, and how to prepare for life beyond graduation while still succeeding in your courses.

PART EIGHT

Academic Relationships, Communication, and Campus Life

University is not only books, assignments, and exams. It is also people. Lecturers, tutors, librarians, classmates, administrators, supervisors, and sometimes employers. Your academic success depends on how you work with people, not only how you study alone.

Many students underestimate this. They think, "If I just read and write, I will be fine." Then they face confusion about an assignment, a registration issue, a missing grade, a group project conflict, or a reference letter request, and they realize that academic life is also social and administrative.

This part teaches you how to communicate like a serious student, how to build relationships that support your learning, how to use campus systems, and how to carry yourself with maturity. These skills protect your grades, your time, and your reputation.

I learned the value of clear communication under pressure. When internet is expensive and unstable, you cannot afford long back-and-forth emails. When power is unreliable, you cannot wait until the last hour to ask a question. You learn to write clearly, ask early, and keep records. These habits help in any country, any campus, and any discipline.

Why relationships matter in academic life

Academic work is assessed by humans. Your paper is graded by a person. Your project is supervised by a person. Your extension request is approved or denied by a person. Your scholarship application is reviewed by a committee. Your reference letter is written by someone who must remember you.

This does not mean you should beg or manipulate. It means you should treat academic life as professional life.

A professional student is not the loudest. A professional student is the one who is:

- Respectful
- Clear
- Reliable
- Prepared
- Honest
- Consistent

When lecturers and tutors see these qualities, they trust you. Trust reduces friction. Friction steals time and energy.

Understanding the roles around you

If you understand who does what, you stop wasting time sending the wrong request to the wrong person.

Lecturer or professor

Usually responsible for course design, lectures, and overall assessment standards. They may not answer instantly, but they can clarify expectations and key directions.

Tutor or teaching assistant

Often handles tutorials, discussions, marking assistance, and practical guidance. Tutors are usually your first contact for weekly learning problems.

Course coordinator

Handles administration and policy within the course. If you have a complex issue, the coordinator may be the right person.

Librarian

Not only a person who gives books. A librarian can teach you how to use databases, find journals, and improve search skills.

Writing center staff

Helps with structure, clarity, thesis statements, and academic writing habits. They do not write for you. They help you write better.

Academic advisor

Helps with course planning, graduation requirements, and academic decisions.

Registrar or administrative office

Handles registration, transcripts, fees, official records, and policy procedures.

Student support and counseling

Helps with stress, mental health, crisis support, disability support, and sometimes learning support.

Knowing these roles saves you time. It also reduces embarrassment. You look serious when you approach the right person with the right question.

Email: how serious students write

Email is one of the fastest ways to gain or lose respect.

A strong email is short, clear, and complete. It does not carry drama. It does not carry long emotional stories. It carries the necessary information and one clear request.

A strong email structure

- **Subject line:** Course code + short purpose
  Example: "POL101: Clarification on Essay Question 2"

- **Greeting:** Use the person's title if you know it
  "Dear Dr. Ahmed,"
  "Hello Ms. James,"

- **One short opening line:**
  "I hope you are well."

- **Direct message:**
  State the issue and the request.

- **Evidence or detail:**
  Mention the assignment title, due date, and the part you are confused about.

- **Closing:**
  "Thank you for your time."
  "Kind regards,"
  Your full name
  Your student ID (if your school uses it)
  Your course section (if relevant)

What to avoid in academic emails

- Long complaints
- Blaming language
- Unclear requests like "help me" without specifics
- Sending messages without your name or course code
- Writing late at night and expecting instant replies
- Sending the same email repeatedly in one day

A practical habit that prevents confusion

Keep a folder for each course in your email. Save important messages. If a policy or deadline was stated in email, you will need it later.

This is even more important when your internet is unstable. If you lose access for a day, you still need your records when power returns.

Asking questions in class without fear

Many students stay silent because they fear looking foolish. But silence is expensive. You lose understanding, then you lose marks.

A mature student learns to ask clean questions.

How to ask a good question

1. State what you understood so far
2. State what is unclear
3. Ask one focused question

Example:
"I understand that the essay needs comparison between two theories. I am unclear about whether we must apply them to one case study or to multiple examples. Should we focus on one case study only?"

That question is respectful and clear. It saves time. It also shows you tried before asking.

If you are shy

Use a small goal. Speak once per week. Ask one question per tutorial. Your confidence will grow through repetition, not through waiting.

Office hours: how to use them like a serious student

Office hours are one of the strongest resources students ignore.

Many students think office hours are only for top students or for students who are failing. Both beliefs are wrong.

Office hours are for clarity and direction.

What to bring to office hours

The assignment question

- The rubric

- Your outline
- Your thesis statement
- One paragraph you want feedback on
- A short list of questions

What to say

Do not say, "I do not understand anything." Say, "I want to confirm if my thesis and outline match the question."

Or, "I am deciding between two angles. Which one fits the rubric better?"

A lecturer can help you quickly when you bring something concrete.

A mistake to avoid

Do not ask for a full review of a long draft at the last minute. Many lecturers will refuse, and even if they accept, the feedback will be limited. Start early and bring small parts.

Tutorial participation and academic maturity

Tutorials are not entertainment. They are practice. They are where you learn how to speak like an academic and how to test your understanding.

A simple tutorial preparation routine

- Read the tutorial questions
- Skim the required reading
- Write 3 short notes:

o   One key idea
o   One example
o   One question

Bring those notes. Speak once. Ask your question. This habit compounds. In a few weeks, you will notice that you understand faster.

Building relationships with lecturers without acting fake

Some students try to build relationships by flattery. That usually fails. Academics can smell fake behavior.

The real way to build a strong academic relationship is simple:

- Attend consistently
- Do the reading often
- Submit on time
- Ask thoughtful questions
- Use feedback
- Show improvement
- Communicate respectfully

Lecturers remember students who improve. They remember students who are serious, not students who are loud.

A reference letter is often given to students who did these things quietly over time.

How to handle feedback without becoming emotional

Feedback can sting. That is normal. But if you respond with ego, you lose the lesson.

How to process feedback

1. Read the feedback once. Do not argue in your mind.
2. Leave it for a few hours.
3. Read it again with a pen.
4. Extract the repeated issues into a personal list.
5. Choose one issue to fix in the next assignment.

This turns feedback into training.

A strong student does not need praise to grow. A strong student needs direction, and feedback provides it.

Classmates: choosing study partners and avoiding academic poison

Your classmates can lift you or drain you.

Some peers will help you grow. Others will invite you into laziness, gossip, and excuses.

Choose wisely.

Signs of good study partners

- They show up
- They share notes when someone misses class
- They discuss ideas, not only complaints
- They respect deadlines

- They do not push cheating
- They speak about improvement, not only suffering

Signs of academic poison

- Constant complaints without action
- Mocking serious students
- Pushing shortcuts and copying
- Turning study groups into social talk
- Blaming lecturers for everything
- Distracting others during exam season

This choice affects your grades more than you think.

Study groups: how to make them work

Study groups work when they have structure.

A strong study group is a training session, not a friendship hangout.

A simple study group structure

- Meet for 60 to 90 minutes
- Set a clear agenda at the start
- Each person explains one topic for 5 to 10 minutes
- Practice 3 to 5 questions together
- End with a list of what each person will do next

A rule that prevents waste

No phones during the study block unless used for course material.

How to handle a weak study group

If a group does not work, leave politely and form a new one. Your time is valuable.

Group assignments: professionalism under pressure

Group assignments teach skills that matter after graduation: coordination, communication, accountability, and conflict management.

They also create conflict when no system exists.

The first meeting should produce five items

1. Roles
2. Internal deadlines
3. One shared document system
4. Quality standard (use the rubric)
5. Communication rule (how often you check in)

Roles that help

- Coordinator
- Researcher(S)
- Writer(S)
- Editor
- Presenter
- Reference checker

One person can hold more than one role, but roles must exist.

Internal deadlines

Your internal deadline should be earlier than the official deadline. That gives room for revision and emergencies.

A simple quality rule

Nothing goes into the final draft without review by at least one other group member.

Handling conflict

Address problems early. Speak directly but respectfully. Avoid gossip. Keep records of agreements. If someone disappears, document your attempts to contact them.

Group work becomes easier when the group acts like a team with rules.

Using campus support services like a serious student

Support services exist because universities know students struggle.

The serious student uses support early, not only after damage is done.

Library support

Ask librarians how to:

- Use databases
- Find peer-reviewed sources
- Use keywords effectively
- Access journals through the campus system

- Request books from other libraries if your campus offers it

If you learn this once, your research becomes faster for years.

Writing center support

Use the writing center to improve:

- Thesis statements
- Paragraph structure
- Clarity and flow
- Referencing habits
- Editing routines

Do not go there asking them to write. Go there asking them to train you.

Academic advising

Use advising to plan:

- Course selection
- Workload balance
- Graduation requirements
- Major or program decisions

Many students lose time by taking wrong courses because they did not ask early.

Counseling and well-being support

If stress, grief, anxiety, or exhaustion is heavy, do not pretend you are made of stone. Get support. Your brain is your tool. Protect it.

Managing your reputation as a student

Your reputation is built daily. It is built through small things.

- Do you submit on time?
- Do you communicate early when problems arise?
- Do you participate respectfully?
- Do you take responsibility for mistakes?
- Do you keep academic honesty?

A student with a strong reputation gets more opportunities: research assistance roles, recommendations, leadership roles, scholarship support, and mentorship.

A student with a damaged reputation faces silent barriers.

Reputation is not about popularity. It is about reliability.

Handling extensions and academic difficulties with honesty

Life happens. Illness, family emergencies, power issues, financial pressure, conflict, and displacement can disrupt study.

A serious student does not hide. They communicate early.

How to request an extension properly

- Request early, not on the due date
- State the reason briefly
- Propose a realistic new deadline
- Attach evidence if your school requires it
- Remain respectful

Do not write long emotional stories. Keep it professional.

If your reason is technology and power problems

Be honest. But also show that you have a plan. For example:
"I have been working offline and I can submit a draft by tomorrow, but I need two extra days to finalize citations and upload due to connection disruptions."

That shows responsibility.

I know how technology limits can disrupt study. When your internet depends on a generator or you rely on mobile data that finishes too fast, you learn to work offline and communicate early. That habit turns hardship into manageable delays instead of failure.

Campus life: balancing academics and social life

University includes social life. Friendships, clubs, sports, events, relationships. These can enrich you. They can also destroy your grades if you lose control.

Balance is not moral talk. Balance is time protection.

A simple balance rule

Do your academic work first, then enjoy social time with a free mind.

If you reverse it, you carry guilt into social life and panic into academic life.

Choose activities that build you

Some clubs build leadership, skills, and networks. Some drain your energy. Choose carefully.

A strong student does not join everything. They choose a few meaningful commitments and do them well.

Leadership and student opportunities

Universities often offer opportunities beyond classes:

- Student government
- Academic societies
- Debate clubs
- Research seminars
- Volunteering
- Peer mentoring
- Tutoring roles

These opportunities can strengthen your resume and your skills.

But do not let leadership replace study. Leadership must serve your future, not sabotage your grades.

A useful approach

In your first semester, focus on learning the system. In your second semester, add one meaningful activity. Later, add more if your grades and energy can handle it.

Professional growth while still a student

University is preparation for life beyond graduation. Many students wait until final year to think about careers. That is a mistake.

You do not need to know your final destination in first year, but you should build useful habits early.

Build your skills in visible form

- Keep your best assignments in a folder
- Keep your best presentations
- Keep your research notes and summaries
- Keep evidence of projects and group work
- Keep certificates from workshops

This becomes your portfolio. A portfolio is proof, not talk.

Build a simple CV early

Even if you are not applying now, build it. Update it each semester. Add roles and achievements while you still remember them.

Learn how references work

A reference letter is not magic. It is built through relationship and performance.

If you want a strong reference later:

- Attend
- Participate
- Submit good work
- Ask for feedback
- Show improvement
- Occasionally speak with the lecturer during office hours

Then when you request a letter, you are not a stranger.

Networking without acting like a salesperson

Networking does not mean pushing yourself into people's faces. It means building real connections through shared work and respect.

Simple networking actions

- Attend a department seminar and ask one question
- Introduce yourself to a guest speaker after the talk
- Join a student society linked to your field
- Volunteer at one academic event
- Ask a lecturer about research opportunities

One clean conversation can open doors later.

Conferences, workshops, and academic events

Even if you are an undergraduate, attend academic events when possible. You will learn:

- What real research looks like

- How scholars speak and argue
- What topics are being studied
- How to present ideas clearly
- How to ask questions with confidence

If you take notes during these events, you gain extra learning that many classmates never touch.

Digital discipline: phones, distractions, and attention

Campus life comes with digital temptation. Social media, short videos, constant messages, drama. These steal attention, and attention is your academic currency.

Practical discipline steps

- Study with phone on silent or in another room
- Use short study blocks with breaks
- Keep one device for studying when possible
- Turn off notifications during study time
- Do not start your day with social media if you have classes or reading

This is not about being strict. It is about protecting your mind.

Dealing with academic pressure and identity

Some students face pressure from family, community, or personal expectations. Others face pressure from feeling behind, feeling poor, or feeling like they do not belong.

These pressures can produce shame. Shame can produce silence. Silence can produce failure.

A serious student learns to separate identity from temporary performance.

A low grade is information, not a verdict. A difficult semester is a season, not your whole story.

If you can hold that truth, you become resilient. You keep working, improving, and asking for help when needed.

Academic boundaries and respect

Respect is not weakness. Respect is discipline.

Respect means:

- Do not interrupt in class
- Do not attack classmates
- Do not mock other accents or backgrounds
- Do not spread rumors
- Do not share private group project conflicts publicly
- Do not share lecture recordings or materials in ways that break rules

Your campus is a community. Your behavior affects your future.

Handling unfairness and misunderstandings

Sometimes you will feel treated unfairly. A grade may feel wrong. A tutor may misunderstand your point. A group member may lie about your contribution.

Handle these situations with calm and evidence.

If you dispute a grade

Do not argue emotionally. Do this:

- Reread the rubric
- Identify where you believe marks were lost incorrectly
- Write a short, respectful message
- Ask for clarification or recheck
- Bring specific examples from your paper

Most institutions have a process. Use it.

If you face discrimination or harassment

Document events. Use campus reporting systems. Seek support from student services. Protect yourself. Silence is not always wise.

A personal discipline that protects everything: records

Serious students keep records.

- Keep drafts
- Keep feedback
- Keep submission receipts
- Keep emails about extensions
- Keep group agreements in writing
- Keep file backups

This habit saves you when problems arise.

I learned this not as a luxury habit, but as survival. When power and internet are unstable, a lost file can destroy weeks of work. When connection is weak, you need proof that you submitted. Records protect your work and your peace.

Closing note for Part Eight

University success is not only reading and writing. It is also communication, relationships, and wise use of systems.

When you communicate clearly, use support services, build respectful relationships, manage group work professionally, and protect your attention, your academic life becomes lighter and your results become stronger.

In the next part, we move into long-term academic planning and progression: how to choose courses wisely, how to build a clear academic path, how to prepare for research projects, and how to carry your learning into real life after graduation.

PART NINE

Academic Planning, Progression, and Life After Graduation

Many students treat university like a road where you simply keep walking until someone hands you a degree. That approach creates confusion. You register for random courses. You overload yourself one semester and underload the next. You miss prerequisites. You choose electives that feel easy but do not help your future. You reach final year and suddenly realize you are missing requirements, references, experience, and direction.

A serious student does the opposite. A serious student plans. Not because life will follow the plan perfectly, but because planning gives you control. It gives you options. It reduces expensive mistakes.

If your life conditions are difficult, planning becomes even more important. When your study time depends on power, internet, money, and family demands, you cannot afford chaos. You need a clear path, clear priorities, and a way to keep moving even when conditions are not friendly.

This part shows you how to plan your degree, how to progress steadily, how to prepare for bigger research work, and how to leave university with more than a certificate.

1. Start with the end in mind

Before you choose courses, ask a simple question:

What do I want this degree to do for me?

Not what you want the degree to "mean." What you want it to produce.

Examples:

- I want it to qualify me for a specific profession.
- I want it to prepare me for a master's program.
- I want it to give me strong writing and research skills.
- I want it to give me technical competence and real projects.
- I want it to open opportunities in public service, NGOs, business, or teaching.

You do not need a perfect answer in first year. But you need a direction. Direction shapes your choices.

A student without direction often chooses based on convenience. Then the future becomes harder.

A student with direction chooses with intention, even when the course is challenging, because they see the value.

2. Understand your program requirements early

Every program has requirements. They are not suggestions. They are the contract between you and the institution.

Your program requirements usually include:

- Total credits needed to graduate
- Required core courses

- Elective options and limits
- Prerequisites and course sequences
- Minimum GPA rules
- Residency rules (how many credits must be taken at that institution)
- Capstone or internship requirements

Do not wait until final year to read these. Read them now. Save them. Print them if needed. Keep them in your "degree folder."

A simple habit that saves you later:

Once per semester, compare your completed courses against the graduation requirements and mark what remains.

This prevents surprises.

3. Course sequencing and prerequisites

Many students get stuck because they ignore prerequisites.

A prerequisite is a gate. If you do not pass the gate, you cannot enter the next course.

Some courses are offered only once per year. Missing them can delay your graduation.

Build a course map.

A course map is a simple list that shows:

- Which courses must be taken first
- Which courses depend on others

- Which semesters each course is typically offered

You do not need a fancy chart. A simple table in a notebook works.

If you are in a program where requirements are strict, course mapping is one of the most important skills you can build.

4. Choosing a manageable course load

Students often think course load is only about time. It is also about mental weight.

Two courses can feel heavier than four, depending on what they demand.

When planning your semester, consider:

- Number of reading-heavy courses
- Number of writing-heavy courses
- Number of math or technical courses
- Lab requirements
- Group project requirements
- Work and family responsibilities
- Travel time and logistics
- Your access to internet and study space

A balanced semester usually mixes heavy courses with lighter ones.

A common student mistake is taking too many heavy courses at the same time, then collapsing.

A stronger approach:

Choose one or two heavy courses per semester, then support them with courses that are less intense.

That is not weakness. That is strategy.

5. Your GPA is not your identity, but it matters

Grades do not define your human worth. But grades can define your opportunities.

Many scholarships, internships, graduate programs, and competitive jobs look at GPA.

If you want those opportunities, you must treat GPA like an asset.

This does not mean chasing perfection. It means avoiding careless losses.

The easiest GPA losses come from:

- Late submissions
- Ignoring rubrics
- Weak referencing
- Skipping revision
- Missing classes
- Failing quizzes you could have passed with basic preparation

You do not need genius to avoid these losses. You need discipline and method.

A good target is steady improvement, not sudden miracles.

6. Major, minor, and elective choices

Electives can either strengthen your future or waste your time.

Choose electives with purpose. Ask:

Does this elective strengthen my major skills?
Does it give me a useful complementary skill?
Does it open a new opportunity?
Does it help my research interests?
Does it improve my writing, speaking, or technical ability?

Some students choose electives only because they sound easy. Then they graduate with gaps.

A stronger student chooses electives that create a useful combination.

Examples of useful combinations:

- Public administration + statistics
- Education + psychology
- Business + communication
- Computer science + writing
- International relations + research methods
- Health studies + data analysis

Your goal is not to collect random courses. Your goal is to build a skill profile.

7. Build a personal skill plan alongside your course plan

Your degree plan tells you what courses to take.

Your skill plan tells you what kind of person you are becoming.

A skill plan answers:

- What skills do I want by graduation?
- What evidence will prove I have them?
- What projects will show them?
- What habits will build them?

Examples of valuable graduate skills:

- Clear writing
- Public speaking
- Research literacy
- Data handling
- Teamwork and leadership
- Digital competence
- Project management
- Critical reading
- Ethical reasoning
- Professional communication

These skills do not appear by accident. You must train them.

A simple way to train them is to treat each semester as a skill-building season.

Choose one major skill to improve each semester.

Example:

Semester 1: academic writing clarity
Semester 2: referencing accuracy
Semester 3: presentation skill
Semester 4: research and literature review skill
Semester 5: data analysis basics
Semester 6: professional portfolio building

This method produces a student who grows steadily.

8. Planning for internships, attachments, and field experience

Many programs require internships. Even when not required, internships can make your graduation stronger.

Internships provide:

- Real work experience
- Professional references
- Practical skill training
- Understanding of how your field operates
- Clearer career direction

Do not wait until the last minute to look for internships.

Start early by doing these steps:

- Identify organizations in your field
- Learn their requirements and timelines
- Prepare a basic CV

- Build a simple cover letter template
- Keep a list of projects and skills to mention
- Ask lecturers or advisors about opportunities

If you live in a place where opportunities are competitive or limited, early preparation matters even more.

9. Preparing for major research projects

Many degrees include a capstone, thesis, or final-year project.

Students struggle because they treat research as something that begins in final year.

A better approach is to prepare slowly from early years.

Build a research interest list

Keep a simple list of topics that keep pulling your attention.

As you read and take courses, notice patterns:

1. What issues annoy you?
2. What problems keep repeating in society?
3. What questions keep returning in your mind?
4. What topics make you read more than required?

That list becomes your research seed.

Build a source bank

When you find strong articles or books connected to your interests, save them and record details.

Even saving 20 strong sources over two years can make your final-year work much easier.

Practice small research tasks early

Every essay is practice.

Train yourself to:

- Form a focused research question
- Build a short literature section
- Use credible sources
- Write with structure
- Cite properly

When final-year research arrives, you will not feel like a beginner.

10. Choosing a supervisor or mentor

If your program includes a supervisor, choose wisely.

A supervisor can either lift your work or slow you down.

When choosing, consider:

- Do they work in your topic area?
- Do they respond within a reasonable time?
- Do they give useful feedback?
- Do they have a record of supervising students successfully?
- Do you feel you can communicate with them respectfully and clearly?

A common mistake is choosing a supervisor only because they are famous or powerful. Fame does not guarantee support.

A good supervisor is not the one who flatters you. It is the one who helps you think clearly and write honestly.

Also, respect their time. Come prepared. Bring outlines and questions. Do not arrive empty-handed.

11. The capstone mindset: fewer claims, stronger proof

Final-year projects often fail because students try to solve everything.

A capstone is not meant to fix the whole world. It is meant to show you can do serious inquiry.

Strong capstones usually have:

- A focused question
- A clear method (even if simple)
- Careful use of sources or data
- Honest limits
- Clear conclusions

If you keep your scope realistic, your work becomes stronger.

In places where data access is difficult, scope control is not optional. It is survival. It is better to do a small study well than a huge study badly.

12. Academic writing for publication and public impact

Some students want to publish articles, policy briefs, reports, or blog pieces based on their studies.

That is a powerful goal. It can build your name and open doors.

But publication requires discipline.

If you want to publish:

- Write clearly for your audience
- Keep evidence and citation habits strong
- Avoid exaggeration
- Avoid careless claims
- Build arguments with solid support
- Learn to accept editing without ego

Even if you do not publish in journals, you can publish in:

- University newsletters
- Department magazines
- Student journals
- Conference proceedings
- Reputable blogs
- Policy platforms and think tanks

The point is not popularity. The point is building a public record of serious thinking.

13. Building a portfolio before you graduate

A portfolio is evidence of your skills.

When you graduate, many people will ask:

What can you do?

A certificate answers only part of that question. A portfolio answers it with proof.

Your portfolio can include:

- Your best essays (with lecturer feedback if possible)
- Reports or case studies
- Presentations (slides plus speaking notes)
- Research proposals
- Capstone or thesis summary
- Data projects
- Internship work summaries
- Leadership roles and outcomes
- Certificates from workshops

Keep your portfolio organized by semester.

If your environment makes digital storage risky, keep backups:

- Cloud storage when possible
- External drive
- Offline copies in a safe folder

I learned this lesson through experience. When power and internet are unstable, losing a file is not a small inconvenience. It can ruin weeks. Records and backups are a student's insurance.

14. References and recommendation letters

A recommendation letter is not a gift you ask from a stranger. It is a professional report written by someone who knows your work.

If you want strong letters:

- Perform well in class
- Participate respectfully
- Meet deadlines
- Visit office hours sometimes
- Ask good questions
- Show improvement
- Do at least one substantial project with a lecturer if possible

Then when you request a letter:

- Ask early
- Provide your CV
- Provide your statement of purpose if relevant
- Provide details about what you are applying for
- Remind them of your work in their course
- Give them enough time

Do not request letters two days before a deadline. That is disrespectful and risky.

15. Planning for graduate school

If you want to pursue a master's or PhD, your undergraduate years are your foundation.

Graduate programs often look for:

- Strong grades in relevant courses
- Writing and research ability
- Clear academic interests
- Evidence of discipline
- Strong references
- Sometimes standardized tests or language scores

Start preparing early by:

- Choosing relevant electives
- Improving academic writing
- Building research experience
- Building relationships with lecturers
- Collecting evidence of your work
- Learning how to write personal statements and research proposals

Also, learn what your target programs require and plan backward.

16. Career planning without panic

Many students fear the question, "What will you do after graduation?"

The fear comes from waiting too long to think about it.

Career planning is easier when you do it gradually.

Step one: understand your field's real options

Many degrees lead to more than one path.

Talk to:

- Alumni
- Lecturers
- Professionals in the field
- Internship supervisors
- Career services

Ask what jobs actually exist.

Step two: identify the skills those jobs demand

Then build those skills in your electives, projects, internships, and self-training.

Step three: collect evidence

Evidence is your portfolio, your internship experience, your projects, your references.

Step four: apply early

Do not wait until you graduate to start applying. Many opportunities have long timelines.

17. Money planning and survival planning for students

This is not talked about enough, but it affects academic performance.

If money is tight, your decisions must be strategic.

- Print only what you need
- Use library resources instead of buying everything
- Download readings when you have access, then read offline
- Plan transport costs
- Avoid expensive habits that drain your budget
- Seek scholarships early
- Consider part-time work carefully so it does not destroy your grades

If your internet access depends on mobile data, plan it like a budget item. Batch online work. Do not waste data on long browsing without purpose.

I had to learn this in real terms. When mobile bundles depleted too fast, random internet use became expensive confusion. Batching and offline work became the only rational approach.

18. Graduation audit and the final year trap

In final year, many students are surprised by missing requirements.

Avoid that by doing a graduation audit early.

A graduation audit is simply checking:

- Credit totals
- Required courses completed
- GPA requirements met
- Internship or capstone completed

- Any departmental requirements met
- Any administrative requirements cleared

Do this at least once per year, and twice in your final year.

Also, keep your own records. Do not rely only on system portals.

19. Leaving university with a clear identity

University should not only give you information. It should shape you.

A strong graduate is not only someone who passed exams.

A strong graduate is someone who learned how to:

- Think clearly
- Write with evidence
- Speak with discipline
- Work with others professionally
- Learn independently
- Handle pressure
- Plan and deliver

That is what makes your education valuable in the real world.

Your goal is not to impress people with big words. Your goal is to be useful, reliable, and capable.

Closing note for Part Nine

Planning is a form of power. It is not about controlling life perfectly. It is about reducing avoidable mistakes and increasing opportunities.

When you map your program, balance your course load, build a skill plan, prepare for research early, collect portfolio evidence, and build professional relationships, you graduate stronger.

Next, we will move into front-to-back academic success habits that tie everything together: how to build your personal academic system, how to keep it consistent across semesters, how to recover from setbacks, and how to keep your learning meaningful beyond grades.

PART TEN

Your Personal Academic System and a Life of Learning

Many students collect study tips the way they collect slogans. They hear advice from friends, lecturers, social media, older students, and even strangers. They try one method today, another method tomorrow, and then they wonder why nothing sticks.

The issue is not that the tips are useless. The issue is that scattered tips do not become a system. And without a system, your academic life depends on mood, luck, and pressure.

A system is not something complicated. It is simply a set of repeatable habits that keep you moving even when life is not stable.

If your life has stable power, stable internet, and a quiet home, you can still benefit from a system.

If your life includes weak internet, expensive mobile data, noisy environments, family demands, travel problems, or unstable power, then a system is not optional. It is how you survive semester after semester without breaking.

I learned this the hard way. There were seasons when internet depended on a generator and could be switched off at any time. There were seasons when I used mobile bundles that depleted faster than expected, and I had to choose between research and simple communication. In such seasons, you stop relying on comfort and start relying on method. Method becomes your quiet strength.

This final part brings everything together so you can build a personal academic system that fits your real life, not a fantasy life.

1. The student who wins is the student who repeats

Success in university is not mainly about one powerful week. It is about small, repeated actions.

A student who writes a little each week will outperform a student who writes only in panic week.

A student who reviews lecture notes within 24 hours will outperform a student who waits until exam week.

A student who tracks sources from day one will outperform a student who remembers references by memory.

Repetition beats intensity because repetition produces stability.

And stability produces quality.

2. The "three-file rule" that prevents chaos

Many students lose time because their work is scattered across devices, folders, and random documents. They have one file on their phone, one on a laptop, one on a flash disk, one in an email draft, and one in a messaging app. Then one day the device fails, or power cuts during saving, or the flash disk corrupts, and weeks disappear.

If you want to avoid that pain, adopt the three-file rule for every course.

For each course, keep three main documents:

1. Notes
2. Sources and references
3. Drafts and submissions

Your "Notes" file contains lecture notes, tutorial notes, and your own summaries.

Your "Sources" file contains your source record: full reference details, plus short notes of what each source contributes.

Your "Drafts" file contains your outlines, drafts, final submissions, and the final version you submitted.

If you prefer separate documents for each assignment, that is fine, but keep them inside the same course folder with clear naming.

Simple naming saves you later.

Example naming style:

CourseCode_Notes_Week03
CourseCode_Sources_Assignment1
CourseCode_Assignment1_Draft
CourseCode_Assignment1_Final_Submitted

This rule sounds small, but it prevents many student disasters.

3. One calendar, one deadline list, one weekly plan

Deadlines are not difficult because they are many. Deadlines are difficult because students keep them in their heads instead of on paper.

Your brain is not a storage room. It is a thinking tool. Do not burden it with tracking tasks.

Use three layers:

A calendar

Put deadlines and exam dates there.

A deadline list

Write every assignment title, due date, and weight on one page.

A weekly plan

Each week, plan your study blocks around deadlines and lectures.

When you do this, your stress drops because your mind stops guessing.

This is especially important when your schedule can be disrupted by things outside your control. A week can be lost to power issues, travel, family emergencies, or financial pressure. A student without a plan collapses when that happens. A student with a plan adjusts and continues.

4. Your weekly cycle: capture, consolidate, build

A strong semester is built through a weekly cycle. Without this cycle, you will always feel behind.

A useful weekly cycle has three parts.

Capture

Attend lectures. Take notes. Save readings. Collect key announcements and assessment instructions.

Consolidate

Within 24 hours, rewrite key ideas in your own words. Define key terms. Create short summaries. Write one example per concept.

This step is where learning becomes yours.

Build

Use what you learned to move your assignments forward. Write one paragraph. Add one source note. Improve one section of your outline.

This step is where grades are won.

If you follow this cycle weekly, exam season becomes normal work, not panic.

5. The assignment pipeline: how to move from question to submission

Many students treat assignments like sudden battles. They wait, then they fight, then they collapse, then they recover.

A better approach is to run every assignment through a pipeline.

Here is a pipeline that works across most disciplines.

Step 1: Decode the task

Rewrite the question in your own words. Identify the action word. Identify the limits. Identify the evidence type the course prefers.

Step 2: Build your thesis or main claim

Write your thesis in one or two sentences. If you cannot do this, you are not ready to draft.

Step 3: Build a short outline

List your main points. Make sure each point supports your thesis.

Step 4: Assign evidence to points

Attach sources to each point. If a point has no support, either find support or remove it.

Step 5: Draft the body first

Write paragraphs using the pattern: point, evidence, explanation, link.

Step 6: Draft introduction and conclusion

Write them after the body is clear.

Step 7: Revise in layers

Check answer accuracy, argument clarity, evidence, paragraph unity, sentence clarity, then references.

Step 8: Final checks and submission

Check formatting, citations, reference list, file naming, and submission requirements.

This pipeline protects you from late-night guessing. It also makes your performance predictable.

6. The exam pipeline: study for retrieval, not familiarity

Exams do not reward rereading. They reward recall.

So your exam pipeline should train recall.

Step 1: Build exam notes early

After each lecture, create a short summary that can be used later.

Step 2: Convert notes into questions

Turn headings into questions. Turn definitions into "explain" prompts. Turn key theories into comparison prompts.

Step 3: Practice answering without looking

Write short answers from memory. Speak explanations out loud. Use practice questions.

Step 4: Use spacing across the semester

Review after 1 day, after 3 days, after 7 days, then later again.

Step 5: Use past papers where possible

Past papers show you how questions are framed and what depth is expected.

When you run your exam preparation through this pipeline, your exam performance improves, not because you became magically smart, but because you trained the exact skill exams test.

7. Recovery after a setback

Some students believe that a serious student never fails. That belief is childish.

Setbacks happen. A bad grade happens. A missed reminder happens. A semester with stress happens. A group project conflict happens. Sometimes a whole plan collapses due to life pressure.

What matters is not whether you fall. What matters is whether you know how to recover.

Here is a recovery process that protects your progress.

Step 1: Separate emotion from analysis

A bad grade can hurt. Accept that feeling. But do not let the feeling become your conclusion.

Step 2: Diagnose the real reason
Ask:

Did I answer the question?
Did I follow the action word?
Did I use enough evidence?
Was my structure weak?
Did referencing errors cost marks?
Did I start too late?
Did I ignore feedback from the previous assignment?

Most of the time, the reason is not mysterious.

Step 3: Extract one or two changes

Do not try to fix everything at once. Choose one or two improvements.

Example improvements:

Start earlier and draft body first.
Use the paragraph pattern more consistently.
Do a citation audit before submission.
Reduce quotations and increase explanation.
Spend more time on planning and outline.

Step 4: Apply the change immediately

Apply it in the next assignment. Do not wait for next semester.

Recovery is faster when it is immediate.

A student who learns from setbacks becomes dangerous in a good way. They stop repeating the same mistakes. That is how average students become strong students.

8. Motivation is unreliable, discipline is friendly

Many students wait to feel ready. They wait to feel motivated. They wait to feel confident.

But confidence is not the door. Confidence is the result.

In real academic life, you often begin when you feel tired, distracted, or uncertain. You begin anyway, because you understand that work creates clarity.

A small habit that helps is to build a "start ritual."

Your start ritual might be:

Open your notes.
Rewrite the question.
Write the thesis sentence.
Write the next small step.

When you do this repeatedly, starting becomes less painful. You stop needing a perfect mood to work.

9. Attention is your academic currency

In campus life, distraction is everywhere. Notifications, gossip, short videos, constant messages, and endless browsing.

If your attention is broken, your study time becomes expensive but unproductive.

Protect attention through simple rules:

Study with the phone on silent or in another room.
Use short timed blocks with breaks.

Batch communication tasks.
Avoid social media during study hours.
Keep one clear workspace, even if small.

If your environment is noisy, protect attention through timing and method. Early morning blocks can be powerful. Short blocks can be powerful. Offline blocks can be powerful.

Attention is not something you "have." It is something you defend.

10. The dignity of honest work

Academic life is full of temptation. Shortcuts exist. Copying exists. Paying someone exists. Borrowing someone's work exists.

But shortcuts steal more than grades. They steal the student's self-respect. They also steal growth. When you do not do the thinking yourself, you remain weak, even if your transcript looks good.

Honest work might be slower, but it produces real skill. And real skill stays with you after graduation.

A degree without skill is a paper shield. It looks strong until real life tests it.

So treat integrity as identity. Not as fear. Not as a rule you follow only when being watched.

A serious student is honest even when nobody sees, because they respect themselves.

11. Learning beyond graduation

Graduation is not the end of learning. It is the beginning of self-directed learning.

After university, nobody forces you to read. Nobody forces you to revise. Nobody forces you to improve writing. Nobody forces you to upgrade skills.

So the student who built a system in university becomes a strong adult. The student who relied on panic becomes a confused adult.

Carry these habits beyond graduation:

- Keep reading and taking notes.
- Keep writing, even if short.
- Keep building skills deliberately.
- Keep tracking sources and learning from serious people.
- Keep revising your work, not only producing it.

This is how education turns into long-term power.

12. A final word to the reader

If you read this book while you are in school, I want you to hear this clearly.

You are not behind because you struggle. Many students struggle. You are behind only when you stop trying to improve your method.

If you are in a place where power is unstable, internet is weak, and study space is not quiet, do not conclude that you cannot succeed. Many students in comfortable places waste their opportunities through careless habits. Your limits can become your training ground if you build a method that fits your reality.

I have lived in settings where learning demanded patience, creativity, and stubborn persistence. I have known the frustration of losing connection when you need it most. I have known the pressure of trying to keep progress when conditions do not cooperate. Those moments taught me that method is stronger than mood, and that planning is a form of freedom.

Start small. Repeat. Improve one thing at a time.

That is how you become the student you want to be.

That is also how you become the adult you want to be.

Final Note to the Reader

Thank you for reading Academic Orientation. If you apply even a few of these habits consistently, your academic life will become clearer, steadier, and more rewarding. Do not aim for perfection. Aim for steady improvement. The student who improves wins.

Leave a Review

If this book helped you, please consider leaving a review. It helps other readers find it and it helps me improve future books.

1. What was the most useful idea you learned from this book?

2. What part made your academic life feel more manageable?

3. Who would you recommend this book to, and why?

Stay Connected

Website: www.johnshalom.com
Email: maluthabiel@gmail.com
Phone: +211 927 145 394

Other Books in This Bridge Set

From Student to Scholar
The Shape of a Life
Survive and Work Online
Truth Written Well
The Hard-Place Entrepreneur
A Nation Without Enemies
Poems That Breathe
The Discipline of Meaning
Publish Like a System
When Faith Is Tested

Permissions, Bulk Orders, and Training Use

For permissions, bulk orders, workshops, training programs, or institutional use, please contact:

Website: www.johnshalom.com
Email: maluthabiel@gmail.com
Phone: +211 927 145 394

REFERENCES

Armstrong, K. (2014). *Fields of Blood: Religion and the History of Violence.* Bodley Head.

Barr Sally, Alfred J., Brusaw T, and Oliu E. Water. 2004. *Writing From A to Z. The Easy-to- use Reference Handbook 5th Edition*: McGraw Hill: New York.

Blaikie, N. (2014). *Designing Social Research: The Logic of Anticipation.* Polity Press.

Carr, D. J. (2016). *The Value of Research in Higher Education.* Journal of Higher Education Theory and Practice, 16(2), 5-15.

Fischhoff, B. (2013). *What Have We Learned About Communicating Risks?* American Psychologist, 68(6), 423–424. https://doi.org/10.1037/a0033774

Hesse, B.W. (2019). *Introduction to Qualitative Research Methods: A Guidebook and Resource.* John Wiley & Sons Inc.

Levinas, E. (1987). *Time and the Other.* Duquesne University Press.

Lynch Mary and Smith M. Hadley. 2001. *Reading and Writing in Academic Community.* Prentice Hall: New Jersey.

Malterud, K. (2015). *Reflexivity: A Key Concept in Qualitative Research?* European Journal of Clinical Investigation, 46(Suppl_1), 3-7.

Murray and Sarah Moore. 2010. *The Handbook of Academic Writing: A Fresh Approach.* Open University Press: Great Britain.

Peter C.B. 2010. *A Guide to Academic Writing.* Zapf Chancery: Eldoret, Kenya.

Repko, A., Szostak, R., & Buchberger, M. (2014). *Integrated Assessment of Complex Problems: An Overview.* Springer Science+Business Media New York.

Seyler U. Dorothy. 2006. *Read, Reason, Write.* McGraw Hill: New Yok.

Shields Munling. 2010. *Essay Writing: A Student's Guide.* SAGE: Los Angeles.

Trouillot, M.-R. (1995). *Silencing the Past: Power and the Production of History.* Beacon Press.